THE PLAINS OF HEAVEN

Dawn Robertson

HAYLOFT PUBLISHING LTD
Kirkby Stephen, Cumbria

First published by Casdec Ltd, 1989
This revised and expanded edition by Haylott Publishing Ltd., 2012

Haylott Publishing Ltd, South Stainmore,
Kirkby Stephen, Cumbria, CA17 4DJ

tel: 017683 41568 or 07971 352473
email: books@hayloft.eu
web: www.hayloft.eu

ISBN 1 904524 87 7

A Catalogue record for this book is available from The British Library

Designed, printed and bound in the EU

Papers used by Hayloft are natural, recyclable products made from wood grown in sustainable forests.
The manufacturing processes conform to the environmental regulations of the country of origin.

Distant and high, the tower of Bowes
Like steel upon the anvil glows;
And Stainmore's ridge, behind that lay,
Rich with the spoils of parting day,
In crimson and in gold array'd

Sir Walter Scott, from *Rokeby*

So many people have helped with this book, by freely giving their time to talk about the history of Stainmore and letting me copy photographs. Sadly, many of these people are no longer alive so this second edition is dedicated to the memory of the many generations of people who lived, loved and cared for this wonderful place, and to James and Lizzie for all their help.

John Martin, 1789-1854, painted this picture, called 'The Plains of Heaven' of the view from Stainmore over the Eden Valley, in 1851-53. This is the second picture in Martin's triptych, unlike the others it is characterised by tremendous tranquillity and harmony. In the central panel, The Last Judgement, the good are shown assembling in 'the plains of heaven'. The celestial landscape continues into this picture, representing salvation. Martin included a number of poets and artists among the good, who are seen in white on the crest of the hill in the foreground of the picture. Behind them stretches the deep blue expanse of a heavenly lake, filled by the rushing water of the distant falls, and surrounded by majestic mountain scenery. The painting is now in the Tate Gallery, London.

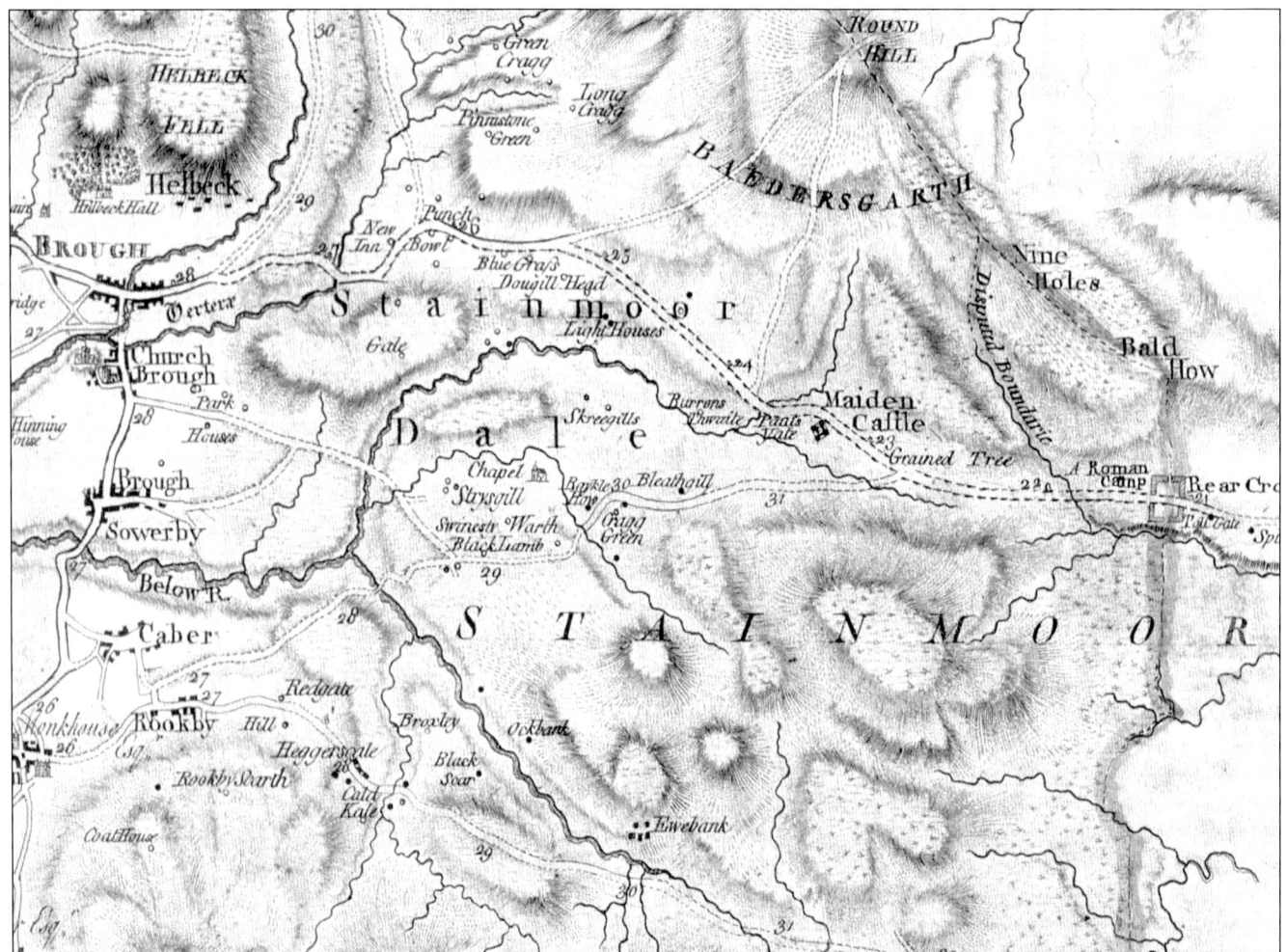

CONTENTS

Opposite T. Jefferys map of 1770, and next page, T. Hodgson's map of 1828, courtesy of the British Library.

EARLY HISTORY

THIS introduction sets out some of the ancient history and legends of Stainmore. The episodes described are mostly those when men and events came to the area, intentionally or by accident, to play out a drama which had begun elsewhere.

This drama begins, in traditional Stainmore spirit, with a lot of snow. Eighteen thousand years ago the Northern Ice Sheet reached its glacial maximum. Glacial ice extended from the North Pole as far as southern Britain. Europe was a permafrost snared steppe. This barren wasteland was inhabited only by the hardiest species of fauna and flora but did have a small human population prepared to brave the fierce northern cold.

Five thousand years later, approximately 11,000BC, global climate change resulted in rapid melting and retreating of the Pleistocene ice sheet. The steppe became fir, larch and birch woodland. Shortly after animals, plants and humans moved north west across a land-bridge spanning the English Channel and connecting south east England with Europe. Deciduous forest crept into Britain and colonised much of the south.

Glacial melt water meant that in 6,500BC the British peninsula permanently became the British Isles as the European land bridge was lost beneath the sea. For the next four millennia humans in the British Isles were largely alone. Stainmore comes into this story when humans reached northern England sometime around 7,000BC. The pass over Stainmore, especially in those frozen days, would have provided an easy traverse across the Pennines.

Ancient British tribes were largely nomadic hunters. A hunter's survival depended on the competence of his weapons. Flint was always the material chosen for arrows, spears, knives and other tools by Mesolithic peoples. Flint had a spiritual as well as practical use, and good flint was traded widely. The eerie green volcanic tuff of Langdale in the Lake District drew people to it and was used for axe making. A trade network existed for distributing this tuff across the British Isles and examples of Langdale stone axes have been found right across Britain and Ireland. The Stainmore Pass has almost certainly been a trade route for thousands of years. During the Neolithic era luxury items became sought after and trade with Continental Europe increased.

Microliths (splinters of flint) are some of the only evidence attributable to ancient human occupation in an area. Flint tools dating from the late Neolithic – early Bronze Age (3000-2500BC) found on Stainmore (see photograph) point to a possible hunting camp, or settlement in the area. Neolithic and Bronze Age Britain heralded changes in culture and ideas based around settled villages and towns supported by agriculture. Kingdoms rose based on natural barriers such as mountains and rivers, Westmorland was probably a small kingdom in its own right by the time of the invasion of the Romans in 43AD.

The remains of old settlements abound in Cumbria, showing traces of prehistoric peoples, and more signs of Bronze and Iron Age farmers. When the Romans, led by Petullius Cerialis, arrived over Stainmore they brought with them sophisticated technology to add to that of the native peoples. The Roman Empire sent out its feelers, controlling the local population and milking the surrounding lands of their mineral and agricultural wealth. They built substantial forts to guard their newly made road over Stainmore which followed the ancient path of Bronze Age traders.

The outline of a large Roman camp can be seen high on Stainmore, while at Brough Castle there was

Flint tools found on Stainmore.

a sizeable fort with associated civilian settlement, and, again on Stainmore a smaller fort, Maiden Castle, guarding the eastern approach to the Eden Valley. Not all Roman buildings had glass but it was essential at Maiden Castle exposed as it was, to the bitter cross Pennine winds. At Roper Castle they built one of a series of signalling stations so that the Romans could signal between Bowes, Brough and further afield to warn, almost as fast as a telephone call, of approaching danger.

The Roman occupation lasted for about 400 years, by which time, no doubt, there had been some mixing of the two peoples, rulers and ruled. As the empire crumbled from within, Roman rule ended, but the evidence of their occupation almost 2,000 years ago can still be traced to this day.

The forts, villas and roads were abandoned and neglected. The local population must have continued with the crafts and agriculture they had used during the occupation, but they did not seem to take over where the Romans had left off, and the grass must have grown over the Roman pavements and their buildings began to crumble.

The next invasion was not so much of rulers or raiders, but of Vikings who sought places to settle and to farm. Some went as far as Iceland or Greenland, and by comparison the Stainmore climate must have been mild. Over time the Vikings mixed with the locals, and their language mingled with that spoken by the residents, created the Westmorland and Cumberland dialects. The high concentration of Viking names for features of the landscape, especially in the upland areas, indicates the success of the invasion.

This does not mean that there was no conflict. There was treachery, hatred and fighting - the Danish King, Eric Blood-Axe, was killed on Stainmore when King Oswulf turned traitor and aided Maccus, the son of Eric's rival Olaf, to kill him. Professor F M Stenton writes, 'It is possible that Eric may have been attempting an invasion of his lost kingdom, when Oswulf brought about his death, but a battle on the heights of Stainmore... rather suggests the last stand of a deserted King on the border of his country. Nothing is certain beyond the fact that the manner of his death gained him the sympathy of those who recorded it.'

Stainmore was for a time the border between Scotland and England and the Rey Cross is said to have marked this division. It was on the frontier and therefore probably the scene of many a skirmish. It was a strategic point in military terms, as the Romans had recognised, since the Stainmore Pass was an important east-west route.

Dowgill, also spelled Doughyll, could mean Black Valley because of the deep valley, or the coal found nearby, or because of a story told by Nicholson and Burn. They say the valley was black with death as well as coal, 'The Earl of Murray and Lord Douglas [in 1390] after fighting a battle in the neighbourhood of Appleby [at Hoff] in a place to this day called Douglas-Ing... burned Appleby and everything which came in their way up to Stainmore... Whether, however, the brave people of Stainmore checked the invaders as tradition reports various places being deemed the site of their interment, as for instance one near the Gale [Thorneygale], or the rugged nature of the country deterred them from proceeding further cannot now be ascertained.' Battle Hill, near Augill Castle, suggests yet another bloody encounter.

Between the battles and skirmishes life went on in Stainmore and a variety of remains, including marks of former enclosures and signs of early cultivation show that agriculture continued to develop. Whilst predominantly a pastoral area, raising cattle and sheep, the land was also capable of producing cereals, principally oats and bigg (barley). There was surplus production to be sold and in 1330 Brough-under-Stainmore was granted its Market Charter to hold a weekly market on Thursday, plus one four day fair in September.

The year 1745 saw the last battle on English soil at Clifton, near Penrith, when the Duke of Cumberland, nicknamed Butcher Cumberland, harried Bonnie Prince Charlie's retreating army. Stainmore was little affected except that tradition has it that the few precious items of silver were all hidden at Swinstonewath.

The last conflict near to Stainmore was in 1663 when Captain Robert Atkinson of Mallerstang gathered an army of rebels against the repressive Five Mile Act of King Charles II which persecuted non-conformists. The men gathered on Kaber Rigg with the intention of capturing Sir Philip Musgrave, the King's man in Carlisle. The militia were sent from Appleby, the rebels were routed and Captain Atkinson was taken prisoner. Lady Anne Clifford's diary records his punishment, 'The 20th day of August 1664 did the two Judges of Assize for this Northern Circuit come hither to keep the Assizes here, where Robert Atkinson, one of my tenants in Mallerstang, that had been my great enemy, was condemned to be hanged, drawn and quartered, as a traitor to the King, for having had a hand in the late plot and conspiracy, so he was executed accordingly on the first day of the month following.' One story says that the King issued a reprieve to Captain Atkinson and a message was sent from London in all haste. It is said that the rider was delayed on Stainmore which, sadly meant that the reprieve arrived half an hour too late.

One final story from the great coaching days of the eighteenth century, when it seems fear and danger were still strong enough to fuel superstition and magical events. The story was told by an old woman called Bella to Mrs Macquoid who recounts it in her book *About Yorkshire*. Bella, as a young girl, was maid to George Alderson; innkeeper of the Spital on

Stainmore in 1797. One cold October night, George and his son were discussing the large sum of money they had made at Brough Hill fair, which had been stored away in a bedroom cupboard. It was a wild, wet and windy night and, 'Mrs Alderson and Bella sat... spinning by firelight, for the last coach had gone by and the house door was barred and bolted for the night.' There came a knock at the door. Bella opened it to find a bent old lady in a long cloak and hood. The old lady came in but refused food or to have her cloak dried, but sat shivering by the fire saying she would sleep in a chair.

The Aldersons went to bed, leaving Bella and the old lady. Bella tried to make conversation but thought the woman's voice sounded odd; then she noticed a horseman's gaiter under the hem of her skirt. Bella was uneasy and decided to lie on the long settle and pretend to sleep. After a time the old woman stood up, tall and powerful, and took a 'brown withered human hand' from inside the cloak. She put a lighted candle in the hand and walking towards Bella, a male voice spoke:

Let those who rest more deeply sleep;
Let those awake their vigils keep.

Terrified, Bella lay still, eyes tight closed. Then the voice continued:

O hand of glory, shed thy light;
Direct us to our spoil to-night.

and holding the hand up to the window:

Flash out thy light, O skeleton hand
And guide the feet of our misty band.

The cloaked figure unbarred the door and whistled. Then it seemed that he somehow left and the door was again bolted. Bella ran to wake the landlord and his wife, but they wouldn't stir. Suddenly there was banging at the door. The band had arrived... A new thought came to Bella; she raced downstairs and flung a cup of milk which stood on the table, at the hand, extinguishing the flame. At once the Aldersons awoke. The robbers were pounding on the door demanding that the landlord produce his valuables. Young Alderson meanwhile aimed his blunderbuss and fired. The robbers changed their demand and shouted, 'Give up the Hand of Glory and we will not harm you.'

Young Alderson fired another shot and the robbers withdrew. The Aldersons kept the withered hand for some years afterwards. The robbers apparently believed that, 'the hand of an executed criminal, pickled and dried according to a special formula and grasping a candle made of fat from the same source, conferred miraculous powers on its possessor.'

All these strange events, are completely out of the ordinary way of life on Stainmore. In some ways the early history is more interesting with legends, battles, and invaders, the stuff of real 'history', but in another sense they are simply extraordinary facts which had little effect on the common man. The greater part of Stainmore's history is one of quiet changes and ordinary working lives which mostly went unrecorded. These ordinary people, with all their colour and variety, bring history alive. They somehow seem more real and close than the great events of history.

A Thousand Years

THE oldest of the old Stainmore families are the Ewbankes. The name goes back somewhere into the Dark Ages and has given rise to Stainmore's legend of the Headless Horsewoman. Accounts of the events suggest that on the Eden fellsides an almost tribal way of life existed; like the Scottish clans, English chieftains ruled in particular areas, protecting their own and marauding against other clans. Stainmore belonged to one of these Saxon chieftains who was called Dew Banke. He had a fort, possibly at High Ewbanke or as some suggest, near Dowgill. He bickered and fought with the Norman baron from Brough Castle, holding his own against him. Over the fells at Barnard Castle, another Norman baron named Fitz-Barnard lived and ruled. He had an only daughter called Ethel who was very beautiful, as in all the good stories...

The fells of Bowes and Wemmergill were a good hunting ground for stag, grouse and wild boar and both Fitz-Barnard and Dew Banke used these hunting grounds. On one occasion the Norman and Saxon hunting parties met on the moors, quarrelled over hunting rights and fell to blows. Dew Banke's group were the stronger and he took Ethel as a prisoner, back to his fort on Stainmore, from where it was more or less impossible to rescue her without a siege.

The story goes that Fitz-Barnard hadn't enough resources to rescue his daughter and appealed to Ralph de Neville from Raby Castle to help. Meanwhile Dew Banke fell in love with his beautiful prisoner in her blue dress. He treated her kindly and asked her to marry him. Despite the kindness of her treatment Ethel, not surprisingly, refused to marry Dew Banke.

Finally her father, with the help of Ralph de Neville's men, managed to rescue his daughter and in the furious fight that ensued Ethel escaped on a bay horse and galloped for her life. Dew Banke, in a blind anger at her loss, chased after her and with one stroke of his sword cut off her head. So, as the legend goes, "Ethel Fitz-Barnard is still seen at the midnight hour, dressed in blue, and mounted on a bay charger galloping along the road towards her home."

More recently, another Ewbank who was also out hunting created another legend. As he galloped over the moors, following the hounds and "the wild-eyed stag," the chase led him towards Hartley Castle. A poem by John Armstrong tells the tale:

But on like wind, o'er the hill madly speeding,
Rude clump, fence or hollow, no check to his speed,
The old castle towers of Harcla receding,
Nigher to the game at each stretch of his steed.

The rocks that protruded to the iron hoofs flashing,
Each flash a bright beacon from the doom that was laid,
Stag, hounds, and horseman o'er the precipice dashing,
At the bottom lay bleeding, all mangled and dead.

The scene of the calamity has ever afterwards been known as Ewbank Scar.

THE STOCKING DEALERS

The Ewbankes became wealthy farmers and landowners and lived at Borrenthwaite. They converted the farmhouse into a fine house, with walled gardens and servant quarters in the nineteenth century. It was sold in the 1960s and so ended a thousand year association between the Ewbanke family and Stainmore.

The association lives on however in the names of places like Ewbank Scar, Ewbank Park and High Ewbank, which is Stainmore's 'lost' village. At the end of the sevennth century it had about 80 villagers; 100 years later numbers had declined to about 50. The villagers lived by husbandry, mining, shepherding, labouring or knitting.

This combination of work, plus an assortment of lesser trades, allowed Stainmore to support a large population. Many houses must have been crowded with families of nine, ten or eleven people. The reason that they could keep such large families at home seems to be the stocking knitting which employed young and old, men and women alike. In 1787 there were 133 people in Stainmore Parish whose occupation was described as knitting. Most of the full-time knitters were female, but there were exceptions. Richard and Esther Alderson who lived at High Ewbank had seven children and two of the sons, Matthew and Thomas, were stocking knitters.

The knitting industry operated with wool being put out to the knitters by stocking dealers from Brough and Kirkby Stephen. Knitters aged over twelve could earn 2s 6d (12.5p) a week, and under twelve about two shillings a week (10p). Experienced knitters could knit about six pairs a week. The stocking dealers like John Wilson of Brough, who was described as a 'Dyer and Callico Printer and Dealer in White Woollen Stockings' and Abraham Dent of Kirkby Stephen who was a 'Draper, Wine Merchant, Brewer and Dealer in Stockings' sent the stockings by pack horse, often as far afield as London.

Abraham Dent has left accounts and letters relating to his Kirkby Stephen shop where he sold an amazing variety of goods, including nutmeg, tobacco, hats, garters, candles, gun powder, books and medicine. Jonathan Ewbanke of Stainmore went shopping to Abraham Dent's shop. He bought a "pound of Coccoa for 1s in 1763" and "6 Quarts of rum for 9s and a bottle of brandy for 1s 6d." He also bought hops so must have brewed his own beer. In the Ewbanke tradition he met tragedy involving a horse, as a tombstone in Brough churchyard tells, "Here lies the body of Jonathan Ewbanke of Little Skirrigill who was unfortunately killed by a fall from his horse, the 12th Dec 1776, aged 49."

Many of the stockings knit by the hands of Stainmore folk ended up on the legs of soldiers. Abraham Dent, for instance, supplied the following stockings to his customer in London in 1767:

Marching Regiment hose at 12s a dozen 420 dozen
Sergeants' hose at 31s a dozen   22 dozen
Mariners' hose at 13s 6d a dozen   132 dozen.

Pictured left, Elizabeth, daughter of John and Rosey Coates who came from Swaledale to live at Palliard. She was born in 1847 and married Joseph Nicholson of High Dowgill. The Nicholson family had lived on Stainmore for over 250 years at Dowgill. Joseph and Elizabeth had six children - two sons and four daughters. Elizabeth is knitting in a tradition which had shrunk by this time from the production of goods for sale to meeting the family's needs in jumpers, hats, stockings, mittens and gloves. She died in 1932 at the age of 85 at the home of her daughter, Mary Jane Dent of Windmore End. Photograph by kind permission of Mr Trevor Dent.

Pictured left, the Dent children from Windmore End, circa 1911. From left to right, Dinah, Joseph William and Bessy, who were the children of John Joseph and Mary Jane Dent. Photograph by kind permission of Mr Trevor Dent, Brough.

According to Sir Daniel Fleming, the knitting industry began sometime before 1671; he writes of Kirkby Stephen, "the market in this Towne is much improved by the Trade of stockings, lately taken up and made in this Towne and parts adjacent." The invention of knitting machines meant that gradually the hand knitters were not needed and by 1842 Poet Close says of Kirkby Stephen Stocking Market, "Here are a few coarse woollen, cotton, knit hose, etc. manufacturers; but this sort of employ and trade hath fallen greatly into decay.'

Apart from the hand knitters the industry provided work for some other related trades like spinning, spinning wheel manufacturers, dyers and soap makers. Anthony Cleasby of Brownhow on Stainmore (a house now long abandoned) was a soap maker and his will of 1708 gives a fascinating glimpse into his trade which he combined with farming. The inventory lists:

	£ s d
His Purse and Apparel	*3.00.00*
Six Steers	*14.10.11*

A Cow and a Calf	*2.06.08*
A Foal	*1.00.00*
Three Spades and a Hammer	*5.00*
A Tubb and a Copper Laddle	*10.00*
Tallow four Hundred Wht	*4.15.00*
Oyl and Pott Ashes	*10.00*
A Stone Saw and Weigh Scales	*2.00*
Owed by Thomas Devis to ye deceased	*1.04.00*
	£28.03.08

A BIT OF BACCY

The decline of the stocking industry and the decline in population occured at the same time and it seems that the two are probably linked. Children would no longer earn their keep at home by knitting and so were sent away as servants or to jobs in the neighbouring towns. The population continued to decline steadily right up to the 1970s when the beginnings of

Photograph right, Christopher and Mary Alderson (née Ellwood) of Oak Bank, South Stainmore, circa 1916. Christopher Alderson was the son of Mr and Mrs James Alderson of Oak Bank - the Aldersons lived at this farm for 100 years. Christopher later moved to Barras Farm where his grandson still farms. Oak Bank is first mentioned in 1700 as Aick Bancke. Photograph by kind pemission of Mr Atkinson, Murton.

a repopulation based on small rural industries and better communication systems seems to have begun.

Knitting continued to be a popular occupation because until the growth of mass produced clothes and shoes, the Stainmore wife would make most of the family's clothes. It was more important to be warm and dry than fashionable, and as Henry Dixon recalls, "There was plenty of foawk used to wear a sack over their shoulders, tied wid a nail. They'd put a nail through and pin them baithe together... it kept you warm and dry, if it was raining it kept a lot of water off... it was a wonder what a sack would turn."

Many of Stainmore's family names continue to this day, while others have long since disappeared, Three hundred years ago the following surnames could be found on Stainmore: Waller, Bonson,

---

Pictured opposite, Robert and Dinah Dent came from Grains o'the Beck, Romaldkirk, to Windmore End on Stainmore before 1850. They had a large family, including Ralph who went to Wyoming and then returned to Stainmore. This photograph shows four generations of the family, taken in about 1930. Back row: Emily and baby Isaac, her husband Joseph with Trevor; grandfather John Joseph, his wife Mary Jane and Aunt Elizabeth. Front row: great-grandmother Elizabeth and Aunt Mary. Photograph by kind permission of Mr Trevor Dent, Brough.

Cleasby, Aary, Johnson, Waistell, Hoops, Eubanck, Nicholson, Brunskill, Alderson, Robson, Bovell, Hilton, Shaw, Devis, Thompson, Dent, Bousfield, Jackson, Wilkinson, Addison, Haistwhittle, Morland, Buckle, Dickinson, Harrison, Loadman, Bails, Varley, Rakestraw, Rud and Bird. Many families had a very long connection with particular houses; for instance the Nicholsons of Low, West and High Dowgill. The last of the Nicholson family has now left Stainmore. One of her memories of the 1947 winter was particularly vivid:

In the 1947 storm, it was a terrible time was that, oh it was frightening, it really was frightening... and one night, the wind got up, and we were sat in the kitchen by the fire and this terrible gale was blowing and I said, "Oh Bob, what's going to happen?"

He said, "I don't know, it's a terrible night."

And you know, there was something at the window, and I said to Bob... and he got up and pulled the curtain by, and you know, the window was sort of frozen, but with having a good fire it had sort of thawed the frost a bit, and you could just see poor Alwyn Glover, he had a balaclava on... and he says, "Has't got a bit o' bacca, Bob?"

Do you know I can hear him saying that yet... he'd walked up from Gillbank, he was so keen to

Ralph Joseph Dent, born in 1862, at Windmore End, had five brothers. The farm could not support six sons, so several of them emigrated, along with many other Westmorland farmers' sons to Australia, New Zealand or America. Ralph went to Wyoming where he worked as a shepherd; many of the emigrants were never heard of again. Ralph decided to return and he farmed at Seavyrigg, high on the fells, and later at Brough Lane Head. This photograph was taken at about the time of Ralph's marriage to Mary Hannah Towers, in 1910. The horse, a typical Dales farm horse, was called Ginger. Photograph by kind permission of Mr Trevor Dent, Brough.

have a smoke! You see, you couldn't get out for shopping, and Bob says, "Well I'll give thee half of what I've got." ...It was twist they used to smoke... and he managed to get the front door open and give Alwyn this baccy.

The closeness of community, helping each other through the hardships of ill health, bad weather or time of shortage, comes out again and again in peoples' stories of old Stainmore. Everyone knew each other and each others' circumstances; there was no need of daily papers to keep everyone in touch, as Mrs Pickersgill explained:

Tommy Sanderson used to farm Gillses as well... and he used to walk up every morning from Skerrygill to Gillses and John Anthony Dixon from Upmanhowe, he'd have been across to the Vicarage, watering etc. and they generally used to meet and they used to sit, for at least an hour in the morning and they were known as the 'Daily Mail'... all the gossip, and in those days, going way back, there was some gossip.

Pictured right, Joseph W. Dent and his wife Emily with Trevor and Isaac Dent, who later farmed at Brampton, near Appleby.

The bridge over the Argill Beck down below Low Dowgill is still there and has altered very little. There are lovely walks among bluebell woods just over the bridge on the Cumbria Wildlife Trust land. In this photograph, from left to right are: Robert Bracken; Dorothy Bracken; Ella Westgarth; Mrs Westgarth and Sally Greenop. Photograph by kind permission of Mrs Pickersgill, (née Westgarth).

The Walker family from Thorneyscales in 1916, from left to right, Annie, Joseph and Mary, cousins of the Walkers from Swinstone House. Photograph by kind permission of Mrs Pickersgill, Penrith.

Photograph above, this was the wedding of Margaret Annie Walker and Wilfred Buckle in April 1922 at Swinstone House. On the back row are, left to right, the bride's parents Mr and Mrs Walker, Joseph her brother, and Elsie Buckle the groom's sister. On the front row is Mary Jane Waller from Bowderdale; the groom and the bride and Ted Buckle, the groom's brother. The Buckles farmed at this time at Bluegrass. William and Annie later moved to Rampson Farm. The family now farm at Buckles and at Bleathgill Farms. Photograph by kind permission of Mrs. Pickersgill.

There was always time to talk and knowing everyone and minding their business or caring about them, had other functions as Mr Bainbridge explained: "In a country place, everybody knows everybody... and if anybody made a slip everybody would know it."

There was hardly a need for a police force to keep order on Stainmore: close rural communities in the past tended to police themselves.

Stainmore people have always seemed to have an independent attitude to any situation. They formed their own conclusions, for better or worse. As far back as the days of Cromwell this tendency to free thinking was apparent. Mr Bird, a corn-dealer from Stainmore, took himself to strongly Royalist Appleby to declare Cromwell's 'Charter of Restriction.' The Rev Machell from Kirkby Thore commented that Bird came from Kirkby Stephen, 'that nest of all traitors!'

Mr Atkinson's father displayed the same individual spirit when he came to keep game for Lord Hothfield at Tufton Lodge in 1896. He said, 'Appleby Castle wanted my father to vote Conservative and he said, "I've always pleased myself, and I always will."'

Pictured right, Harry Atkinson who lived at Tufton Lodge for many years and worked as a gamekeeper.

The Dent family of High Ewbank, photographed in around 1900. William Dent, farmed at High Ewbank and he and his wife Elizabeth, had ten children - five boys and five girls. Three generations of the Dent family farmed at High Ewbank for over a century. George William, the tall young man in the centre of the photograph is the father of George Dent of Winton who kindly loaned this photograph.

Agriculture

IF the history of Stainmore was a film, from creation onwards, people would only appear in the closing reel. The story of millions of years of gradual change can be read in the formation of rocks. Stainmore has in turn been covered by warm seas and by hundreds of feet of ice. The seas left the limestone and sandstone. The glaciers bulldozed mountains, pushing rocks for many miles. Then, as they melted, the ice cold water carved some of Stainmore's deep gills. The glacier deposited some of its load of debris including huge lumps of granite knocked off the top of Shap Fell.

The most recent geological period has seen the formation of a thick layer of peat on the higher ground, up to three metres deep in places. Throughout this layer lie the remains of Stainmore Forest, which was mostly birch. The tree cover gradually declined to be replaced by peat forming mosses and heathers.

The first Stainmore farmers probably lived in clearings in the forest where the wild boars and wolves still howled. The local population, and later settlers, like the Vikings, began gradually to clear and improve the land. Generation after generation have cleared stones and drained the land; the process has never been finished as some boulders proved too massive to move. Trees and scrubland were rooted out to create fields, though again the job was never completed and some of the woodland seems to be the last remnants of the ancient Stainmore Forest.

Before the Norman Conquest there is evidence of a Saxon Chieftain ruling Stainmore, but there is no Domesday record to give us even a glimpse of life here nearly a thousand years ago. The Domesday recorder's comments on Westmorland and the other northern counties were that they had been so often laid waste by feuding and battles with tribes to the north, that there was nothing worth recording. Stainmore became the property of the Norman de Veteriponts, then the Cliffords and later the Earls of Thanet, but the overlords were rarely resident so the tenants retained a certain independence of view.

They were not, however, economically independent because of the complicated system of land ownership. To explain the system, one farm, Light Trees, gives an example. In 1770 the freehold was owned by the Earl of Thanet who claimed rent from the farm. The church also had certain monetary claims,

Harvesting near Swinstone, South Stainmore, during the First World War - Stainmore's first cereal crop for some years. From left to right: George Bainbridge, junior; Jack Alderson; Mr George Bainbridge; Mrs Bainbridge; Mrs Jane Atkinson of Tufton Lodge; Mr Walker of Thorneyscales; Mr Arthur Dent; a prisoner of war called Erich; Bob Dent; Jack Walton and Ernie Dent. In the background with the horses are Mr Walker from Swinstone and Jack Bowron. Photograph by kind permission of Mr Atkinson, Murton.

Threshing Day on Stainmore, 1917, in a pasture close to Mouthlock Chapel. The threshing machine was hired to do the job of today's combine harvester. Mrs Beckwith of New Hall is leaning on the gate with one of her girls - either Elsie or Nellie. The children had stopped to watch the machine as they walked home from school. Photograph by kind permission of Mrs Pickersgill.

paid in the form of a tithe. John Waller was the copy-holder who held the customary inheritance of Light Trees, which could be handed down to his son. If he had lived freehold at the farm he would have been described as 'yeoman'.

John Waller was in fact a Purser in the Navy and rented Light Trees to a tenant for 60 guineas a year. The tenant would generally be called 'husbandman', and would probably be liable for rent to all three landlords. This perhaps explains why John Waller has trouble with his tenants and complained, "I do not know why the Stainmore tenants should not pay as well as those at Coat Gill as the tack notes are the same, at least they do not pay agreeable to the promise made in them, so that they have no right of being so exact, and sooner than their doing so, would oblige them to give up their farms." Soon afterwards Mr Waller gave up trying to get his rent and sold the customary inheritance of Light Trees.

FIELD NAMES

The number of farms on Stainmore gradually increased from twelve in the fifteenth century to nearly 100 in the eighteenth century. The areas of enclosed and cultivated fields had spread little by little, taking in all the lower land and extending up the fellsides. The field names are a clue to the earliest enclosures, with ancient sounding names like Sellgraines, Aereal, Peckass, Steering, Jack Trig, Snout, Benty Close, Cuddy Wife, Magma, Rish, Traws and Great Flosh to name a few. Later enclosures tend to have less poetic names - Far Pasture, Home Field, Cow Pasture, High Ground and Intack Allotment. The oldest enclosures take up about one third of the total area of Stainmore parish and are mostly on the lowest land. The farmers came to private agreements to enclose. The newer enclosures tend to be on higher ground and an Act of Parliament was needed before the last of these could be walled in.

The Tithe Map of 1843 shows that Stainmore consisted of 180 acres of arable land, growing wheat, barley and oats; 2,116 acres of meadow; 4,152 acres of pasture and 20 acres of woodland. Added to this there was 16,000 acres of unenclosed common with rights of grazing called stints. The right to keep stock on the common allowed many part-time or small farmers to make a living from a farm of only a few

Reaping corn on Stainmore - front row, left to right, George and Michael Bainbridge, Walter Richardson from Barras-side and Ernest Dent from High Ewbank. Men with horse in background are Mr Walker from Swinstonewath and unknown. Back row, left to right, Arthur Dent, Mr Bell from Rampson, unknown, John Bowron, Annie Buckle (née Walker), Mabel and Mary Bowron from Mouthlock, Mrs Walker and Annie Buckle's child (Evelyn Buckle).

Sheep clipping, 1916, at an allotment above Barras Station, belonging to Mr Walker of Swinstone House. The numbers of men involved in the shearing on this photograph are small in comparison to the old 'boon shearings'. From left to right, Mrs Simpson, the station master's wife; unknown; Mr Walker; Mr Oyston; Joseph Walker of Thorneyscales; Len Dixon; Mrs Westgarth, the vicar's wife and Mrs Walker of Swinstone House. Photograph by kind permission of Mrs Pickersgill.

acres of enclosed fields. When part of East Stainmore Common was to be enclosed in 1899, it took an Enclosure Act to sort out the knotty problem of ownership and rights of stint.

It may seem surprising that the upland pastures of Stainmore could support any arable production. There is plenty of evidence to show that apart from cattle and sheep, arable crops were also grown. In many fields the medieval marks of rig and furrow are obvious. The field names themselves show former usage, for example, Far Cornfield, Corn Close, Grains and Great Ploughing.

In the 1780s Abraham Dent was buying wheat from John Ellison of Barras Hall, and at this time there was also a corn mill, Oxenthwaite Mill, near Buckles Bridge. The mill race and outline of the building can still be seen. The mill continued to operate until the 1830s when James Parkin, the miller, and his family moved out. Oxenthwaite Mill must have stopped grinding corn as the next occupants were Richard Hunter, a clog maker, and his family. There may have been another corn mill near New Hall, as two millers and their families are listed living on South Stainmore in 1787.

Arable crops on Stainmore became less and less economic and were almost unheard of when, "In l916 orders came that Stainmore had to plough out and grow corn." The farmers shook their heads in doubt, but it had always been possible, if difficult, to grow wheat, barley and oats on Stainmore. They carried out the orders and the war-time harvests were a success, as the photographs in this chapter show.

DUAL INCOMES

Farming on Stainmore was never easy and, although there are exceptions, it tended to provide a living but no more. For this reason many farmers had another job, for instance there are farmers who also worked as weavers, miners, masons or innkeepers. The farmer also relied upon his family to produce his labour force, and only if he had no children or his children were very young would he employ servants. In 1787 for instance, Richard Brunskill of Gillses had three children under six, so he employed William Brown, aged 22, for 'husbandry' and Mary Nelson, aged eighteen, for 'drudgery'!

Another farmer, William Adamthwaite of Spurring End, had seven slightly older children. John who was sixteen was employed in 'husbandry' and William who was twelve was 'shepherding.' His other children were daughters and they were all busy knitting stockings to supplement the family income. Even Agnes, who was only three, was knitting! This dual income economy, with farming supplemented by other industry supported a population of over 600 on a large number of small farms, mostly under 50 acres.

Farming methods at the beginning of the twentieth century were much the same as they had been for centuries and the real agricultural revolution only started with the arrival of the tractor. When older people remember farming before the First, or even the Second World War, they are talking of traditions which are centuries old. The following extracts discuss some aspects of a farming life on Stainmore in the closing days of horse power.

Mrs Buckle remembered, "When we were at Rampson we had no implements... we just had a mowing machine, and we had to do all t'other by hand."

Everything was mended if at all possible, and though this farmer's wife was from Asby, Mrs Alderson, a tinsmith's wife from Appleby explains, "We decided we couldn't make a living out of doing repairs. It was 6d, 6d, 6d and one woman who came from Asby brought an eight pint tin. Joe made them: straight-sided, no lid, you milked into them. And a woman brought this to have a new bottom put in it, and Joe said, 'I'm sorry, but I can't repair it, it's done.' And she said, 'What? We've nobbut had it three and fowty year!'"

WEEKLY ROUTINES

The farmer's wife had a weekly routine - Monday was washing day, Tuesday churning day, Wednesday bedroom day, Thursday baking day and Friday cleaning day. The routine might vary slightly between different farmer's wives and at different times of year, but it was a basic framework to the housework.

Washing was done with, "a poss tub and a mangle. You just possed with a big stick in what we used to call t'cart house, 'twas like a big place where we kept calves and such like, but we had a fireplace. We hadn't a boiler at Swinstone, but we had a good big pan what we used t'heat water with."

There were no gadgets to make cleaning easy. "John's mam used to have this fireside black-leaded, and the floors were flagged, take the mats up and down with a scrub brush and off you went. They even used to wash and scrub the handles of the brushes and the shovels. I've seen my mother scrub these beams with sand and a wet cloth, they used to be white."

Butter was made at every farm, and after milking the cows by hand, the milk was, "set up in bowls and then we'd tek t'cream off. You had it to churn, you had it to warm to a certain degree... We had some [butter] hands you know, and we med it like that, and then we had a bowl and a print and you rolled it around this wooden bowl and med it into a round."

Ploughing on Stainmore

It was hard work, as Mrs Nicholson recalled, "I always remember churning day because A. T. Bird used to come round for the groceries, and I used to be churning and sometimes you couldn't get it to go to butter, and there you were flogging away with this churn, and it would go to sleep. Then you had to keep reversing and trying to shake it... we had all that to do, and then make it up, and you could only get 9d a pound for it."

Stainmore Cheese was made at many houses, including Mouthlock Farm, by Mrs Dixon, "I used to make the morning's milk into cheese and the evening's milk into butter... We used to sell a lot

The war time order had come to grow cereals and potatoes, even on land over 900 feet above sea level. Stainmore farmers obeyed the order, despite the predicted difficulty of growing and harvesting cereals. To the right are Joe Walker, Michael Bainbridge and John Bowron from Mouthlock ploughing a field near the cottage at Low Field. Photographs by kind permission of Mrs Pickersgill.

The first wheat grown high on Stainmore for many years was cut in 1916 near Great Skerrygill. Mr Bell from Rampson Farm is seated on the double mower and Michael Bainbridge from Stricegill, holds the rein. Photograph by kind permission of Mrs Pickersgill.

just locally, they used to come to t'house and buy a whole cheese. There was a lot of work attached to it. When t'milk went into t'house you put it into a big bath in front of t'fire and it had to be a certain stiffness... And then they used to get the cheese off, into a muslin cloth you see. You hang it up to drain and then put it in a cheese vat on a night, after it had drained all day. The vat had holes in it - it went sort of solid and then you used to cut it up and salt it... Then it was in cheese presses, it was weighed... It was very good cheese. You never had very good calves if you made nothing but cheese, so we used to make butter so t'calves got some blue milk."

The pig would get the whey from the cheese and every farmhouse had plenty of home cured bacon. Not everyone liked pig killing time.

Mrs Dixon said, "I remember one year, it was a very, very hard winter and hard frost and we'd killed our pig and it was hanging up in the barn you know, ready to be cut up, and they couldn't possibly do anything with it, it was frozen so hard. Richard Raine used to come up to help him cut it up, and we had to bring the whole carcase into the kitchen and we had a big table in the kitchen and they just had to lay it on the table all night till it thawed out, and then he came another night to cut it up. It was terrible that, having this pig in the house like that... Tommy Sanderson, he was at Skerrygill, he used to come across and kill the

pig you know and he used to say, 'There should be nothing wasted but the squeal.' It was a cruel job was that, killing a pig."

Poultry was almost always kept, with breeds like Rhode Islands, Wyandottes and Leghorns producing both eggs and meat. Before Street House was renamed Hillcrest, Mrs Bailes, who lived in one half of the house, would be seen every morning setting off down the A66, "with about eight or nine ducks, and she would hobble away down the road... to a spring where the water used to bubble up and come out and make sort of a pond, and she used to walk down there with her stick and bring these ducks to the pond. Then at night, when we were leaving school... you'd see her coming down to take them back."

Mutton was another important source of food as Mr Bainbridge recalled, "One of the things they used to do in summertime, three or four farmers would get together and one would kill a sheep this week, you see they could only manage to keep it for so long, and then he shared it with the other three. Now when that meat was finished the next farmer killed a sheep and he shared it; now there's two shoulders and two legs - and if he got a leg off a man then he gave him one back. The sheep weren't all just exactly the same size..."

WHEN FOXES BARK

The weather was all important to farming and before the days of professional forecasting, the farmers did their own. There were many sayings to help the prediction:

> *When t'wind blows hard frae Stowgill east*
> *Ye ma foad yer sheep and hoos yer beyast.*

> *When t'helms load and foxes bark*
> *Bar up your door afore its dark.*

There were predictions concerning sheep:

> *She sets up her back, that old crock yow,*
> *She'll nivver live to hear t'cuckoo.*

And the sheep did their own predicting:

It's funny, sheep are marvellous weather forecasters, out on the moor there... I used to try and get around the moor, get them pulled back if ever I thought there was a storm, to a sheltered place... if it came a storm, they used to come back down into there. You could go up there and do you know 75% of them would be there. But the younger ones that had never been out before, we used to hunt them and bring them back.

Bad weather could ruin the hay crop and that could mean losing stock in winter. Mr Dixon recalls, "It was a very bad haytime in 1946, the worst hay time that ever I seen in my life; we never got no good hay, but I had a stack of real good hay from the year before and that's what kept the sheep alive."

Predicting the weather or making provision for it, made the difference between making a living or making a loss.

Mr Dixon said, "I laughed one morning, I was still lying a bed, and me dad came tearing upstairs and shouted me out. 'Come on, be sharp, Jimmy Coatesworth [from Great Skerrygill] is rowing some hay up.' We shot out of there, well he'd nearly got it rowed up. Me dad said 'It must be going to rain.' We catched t'hoss, rowed some up, and do you know, Jimmy, he rowed his up, and his sister come, and he swept it, and he put t'hay up into pike, and they were just finishing last one off, about 8 o'clock, when it started to rain. They went quietly home and milked... He was about the best weather prophet, was yon man, that I ever knew in my life."

Neighbouring farmers helped each other at busy times of year, especially hay time and sheep shearing. They were friendly and ready to help, which made a hard life easier. Without doubt farming on Stainmore in the days where everything was done by muscle power, whether horse or man, was hard. It was a way

A butter making class at Brough in 1910. Photograph by kind permission of the Beamish Museum, County Durham.

of life, and for some it was the only way of life.

The Eden Valley, it's sometimes called The Garden of Eden, so far as farming's concerned, and even the hills around about it, you're not that far from a better type of land, although Stainmore's hard, I grant you Stainmore's hard. I'm talking about in farming terms. But then you see, to us, being brought up in amongst that, it's a way of life. We hope to make a decent living as we're travelling. It's something that you... well I didn't farm on me own until I came to Stainmore, but it's something I always wanted to do and the only thing I wanted was sheep on a moor, fell sheep, that's the one thing I wanted. I got it at the finish, for the last few years of my life and I enjoyed it.

The main feeling about the days before the tractor revolution seems to be that, "They were happy days, but they were hard days, very hard days."

Tan Hill Swaledale Sheep Show, in the early 1960s. The show was founded in 1951 and is always held on the last Thursday in May. The show is only for Swaledale sheep but also, almost always features the Lofthouse Brass Band. In May 1986, just over six months after Alex and Margaret Baines took over the Tan Hill Inn, they remember that, on show day, local farmers and competitors drank nine gallons of Famous Grouse whisky!

THE GREAT WAR

THE First World War was officially declared on the 28 July 1914. The events that followed shook the western world like no war before it had done. The great and terrible war wasn't to end until the 11 November 1918. No community or household was spared directly or indirectly the spectral presence of this war. Stainmore was no different.

Even in July 1914 the cogs and wheels of the war machine had began to whirr. Factories designed to produce the luxuries of peace were reworked to create the grim necessities of war. Coal was the driving force for the production of armaments. There was a rising demand for Stainmore coal to supply local households as other sources of coal were directed to the war effort. The Great Depression after the First World War also resulted in increased coal production on Stainmore and previously closed mines were re-opened to provide jobs.

Farming has long been a staple occupation on Stainmore. Food like bullets and bombs was a resource critical to the War effort. Because of this farmers were often excluded from conscription and this was true for some of the men of Stainmore. Land on Stainmore that had been used for pastoral farming for many years was turned over to arable farming, and wheat, barley and oats were grown for the war period.

The women of Stainmore took over jobs as men left for the war, and Land Army girls were used on Stainmore. Other women helped by making warm clothes and sending whatever comforts they could to their sons and husbands on the front line. In bigger towns and cities many women were working in factories producing armaments. Without this important work the country would have run out of resources and the war would have been lost.

Photograph right, Land Army girls, 1915, standing in front of the fountain at Borrenthwaite Hall. Every farm had to grow extra food crops and the girls in this photograph were about to go potato picking. From left to right, Florence Eshelby who lived at Borrenthwaite from 1912 to 1930 as a companion maid; Elsie Pratt of Light Trees; Bella Coates also from Light Trees; Elsie's sister; Sally Greenop from Renwick, who was also the school teacher at South Stainmore School. Photograph by kind permission of Mrs Pickersgill.

During the First World War the trains to and from Barras and Kirkby Stephen were disrupted. The girls, pictured above, travelled by train to school, had to leave Barras at 7.30am and return at 8.40pm. Revd. Westgarth organised a horse and tub trap so that their day was not as long. The trap is just passing the Slip Inn. From left to right are Mary Bowron from Mouthlock; Margery Simpson from the Station; Mr Bainbridge the driver; Margaret Dixon; Louise Swinbank of Cragg House and Ella Westgarth.

As the war gained in momentum and all possible resources were directed to the struggle, conscription was introduced. From 1916 onwards young and old were drawn from across the UK and the Empire to quench the war machines thirst. The heaviest blow a community could suffer were the deaths of its young men. Four men from North and two from South Stainmore, were killed. Considering the population of Stainmore at that time these were heavy losses. Their deaths were mourned and marked with memorials in both the North and South Stainmore churches and chapels. In autumn 2010 North Stainmore Chapel was closed and the war memorial in honour of the four local men was moved to South Stainmore Church where it is now kept.

The memorials read as follows:

From North Stainmore:
Private Isaac W. Bousfield, West Riding Regiment, 27 June 1917; Gunner Edward Bousfield, Tank Corps, 31 July 1917; Gunner William E. Bousfield, Royal Field Artillery, 1 June 1918 and Private William H. Sowerby, Durham Light Infantry, 11 April 1918.

From South Stainmore:
In memory of George Alderson of Calva and George Alderson of Barras, men of this parish who

Annie Walker, at Swinstone House, in about 1915. Her brother Joe was in the Navy during the Great War and Annie is wearing his uniform. Photograph by kind permission of Mrs Pickersgill.

Pictured above, Constance Annie Dalston-Ewbank, in 1915, aged eighteen. Constance worked as a nurse during the war and was the daughter of Dr and Mrs Dalston-Ewbank of Borrenthwaite Hall. Her brother George served in the First World War.

Pictured right, Sgt. Robert Davidson of Oxenthwaite with an unknown colleague, also a sergeant in the Border Regiment.

gave their lives in defence of Righteousness and Freedom in the Great War, 1914-1918. This Memorial window given by parishoners and others interested in the parish of Stainmore was dedicated 1st June 1923 by Herbert, Lord Bishop of Carlisle in grateful rememberance of George Alderson of Calva, 6th Battalion the Border Regiment, born 3rd February 1896 at Skerrygill, died 7th October 1917 of wounds received in action in Flanders, buried in Mendinghem Military Cemetery near Poperinghe. And George Alderson of Barras, 3rd Battalion, Loyal North Lancashire Regiment, born 20th May 1897 at Oakbank, died from results of service, 19th September 1919 at Barras.

Some men from Stainmore did return after the War, but all were changed forever by the experience. Jimmy Coatesworth, for instance, suffered for the rest of his life from the effects of mustard gas. Robert Davidson (the author's great-grandfather) was a gamekeeper on Stainmore and a father of two. He was called up during conscription and at the age of 36 fought in France on the Somme as a Sergeant in the Royal Artillery, Border Regiment. As a gamekeeper before the war he used firearms often, but after the war, for the rest of his life, he never fired a weapon again and he would never speak a word about his experiences.

George Alderson of Calva Farm served in the Border Regiment during the war. His parents George and Margaret Anne Alderson (née Cleasby) were married in 1890. They farmed at Calva until 1939 when they moved to Duckintree. They had three children - Mary, Cleasby and George. Their youngest son, George, pictured above, was killed in the trenches. Photograph by kind permission of Mrs Pickersgill.

49

This photograph was taken in 1917 at South Stainmore School where local people organised a Red Cross Sale to raise money for the troops. On the photograph are Mrs Dalston-Ewbank, her son George, and the vicar's wife, Mrs. Pickering.

Thomas Wilson Bracken, born in 1865 on Stainmore, became a civil engineer in Newcastle-upon-Tyne and in Africa. He wrote articles for the local press and, in 1915, despite being in this 50s he answered the call of duty, and became a Lieutenant and then Captain and served at Arras and Passchendaele.

Whilst in France and Belgium, Captain Bracken visited many towns that had been hit by repeated artillery strikes. In the crumbling wreckage of once magnificent cathedrals and churches in the towns of Ploegstaert, Neuve Eglise and Arras, Captain Bracken found small pieces of broken stained-glass windows. He collected the shards of glass and, when he returned to Stainmore, he gave them to South Stainmore Church to be incorporated into a new west window. The pieces of glass depict the face of an angel, a flower and trefoil foliage. Most are cracked and one of the shards has actually melted and bubbled in the heat of an explosion. Captain Bracken's intention was that some of the spirit of the destroyed holy buildings of France lived on in the chapel.

CHURCH AND CHAPEL

RELIGION, work and play are knit into a tight pattern in the lives of Stainmore people in the past. The further back you look the tighter the pattern and only in recent times have the three begun to unravel somewhat. Mr Bainbridge, late of West Dowgill explains, "Now my first remembrance of it, I'd say about nine out of every ten people attended a place of worship, and most of them would attend twice on a Sunday and at least half of them would go once through the week... since the last War - there was a bit of a change after the First War - but a tremendous change after the last one."

Until the beginning of the seventeenth century Brough was the nearest church and a long trudge from some of the outlying farms. In 1608 the school, founded by Cuthbert Buckle, was consecrated by Bishop Robinson and became St Stephen's Chapel. On Sundays the school master would become curate and take divine service, saving the Stainmore people a long walk to Brough. In 1699 the Earl of Thanet rebuilt the Chapel which had fallen into disrepair, adding a school house to the north side of the building. The curate/school masters of this early period include Robert Cragg, John Bracken, James Fenton, John Mason Fenton and James Sawrey.

James Sawrey appears to have been a man of great energy. The earlier vicars had mostly used an ancient house called Knoway as the Vicarage. In 1837 the Revd. Sawrey built the present Vicarage close to Knoway, planting trees around the house for shelter. He was at this time 35-years-old, unmarried, and described as perpetual curate and farmer of 30 acres. Having tidied up the Vicarage he then set about rebuilding the Church, which was completed in 1842.

Several improvements have since been made to Revd. Sawrey's Church, but the main fabric remains the same. A gallery added by Sawrey was removed in 1879 by Revd. Wharton, who also covered the old flags with floorboards, and added lamps in 1882 to allow evening services to be held. The Revd. John Wharton was a widower from Appleby. He lived with his sister Maria who acted as housekeeper and school governess.

Until 1873 the people of North Stainmore had a long walk to Church, either in Brough or at South Stainmore. The vicar of Brough at that time, the Revd. Lancelot Jefferson, decided to build St Mary's Church opposite the Punch Bowl, at his own expense,

PRIMITIVE CHAPEL, MOUTHLOCK. 1349.

Left, the Primitive Methodist Chapel at Mouthlock, 1908. It was built in 1831, though the Primitive Methodists on Stainmore were established well before this date. Mr Hilton of Mouthlock was one of the founder members and Hugh Bourne, an important Methodist preacher, came at the invitation of Mr Hilton to preach at Mouthlock in 1831. The meeting room was upstairs, with three cottages below, which were used for less well off families, often coal miners. The portion with the gable end towards the camera was built by the railway workers who arrived in the late 1850s and early 1860s. These men also built the Belah Viaduct which can be seen to the left in the background. Photograph by kind permission of Mr and Mrs Bell, Kirkby Stephen.

Pictured right, inside the meeting room at Mouthlock Primitive Methodist Chapel, the room in which Hugh Bourne preached. The photograph was taken shortly before the old chapel was closed in 1909. Photograph by kind permission of Mr and Mrs Bell, Kirkby Stephen.

PRIMITIVE CHAPEL, MOUTHLOCK. 135

PRIMITIVE CHAPEL, MOUTHLOCK.
1363. STONELAYING CEREMONY, JUNE 10TH 1909.

Above, the stone laying ceremony for the new chapel at Mouthlock in 1909, at which £500 was raised towards the cost of building the new Primitive Methodist Chapel. The building cost £800 in total, carting and building stone being provided free by the local farmers and by Mrs Dalston-Ewbanke of Borrenthwaite Hall. Thomas Hilton of Bishop Auckland, descendant of Mr Hilton who helped build the original chapel, won the contract to build the new chapel. The photograph opposite shows the old and new South Stainmore Chapels.

54

for the convenience of North Stainmore parishioners. The Church was deconsecrated and turned into a dwelling towards the end of the twentieth century.

METHODISM

The people of the North Pennines had an early affinity to the Methodist movement. John Wesley travelled and preached in many of the northern villages and towns. In 1766 and again in 1768 he preached at Arthur Johnson's farmhouse near Brough. There was an Arthur Johnson living at Bleathgill at the time which was almost certainly the farmhouse in question. A group was formed, probably about that time, to continue these spiritual ideals. In 1793 the Stainmore Methodist movement was said to have twelve members. They built their first Chapel at Mouthlock in 1831. The Chapel incorporated three small cottages with a meeting room upstairs. In the early census records only two of these cottages were ever occupied; they provided homes for less well off

The new Mouthlock Chapel, at South Stainmore.

The altar of South Stainmore Church in 1911, before restoration work removed the old pews and paraffin lights. The altar window was moved to the back of the Church and when it was moved some pieces of glass were added to the design. The glass had been brought back from France and Belgium during the First World War by Captain Bracken from Rampson Cottage. He had found it amongst the mud and debris of destroyed churches and a cathedral. Photograph by kind permission of Mrs. Pickersgill.

Inside South Stainmore Church in 1911. The building was neglected after the Revd. Lax affair. The old pews were painted and the black leaded cast iron stove provided heating. Photograph by kind permission of Mrs Pickersgill, the Revd. Thomas Westgarth's daughter.

families, older people, widows, coal miners, labourers, limeburners, shepherds and later railway workers.

South Stainmore Chapel at Mouthlock was built in 1909 by public subscription to provide more room than the former Chapel a few yards away. It cost £800 in total with much of the work and building materials being supplied free by local people. Mr Atkinson from Tufton Lodge, remembers how he would spend Sunday as a boy at this Chapel.

"We used to go to the Sunday School on a morning, tek a few sandwiches with us. Old Joe Dent was in charge, from Cragg Green. He'd mek us a drink of tea. We used to stop at Chapel in the afternoon, go home, get our teas and then come back at night with father and mother."

North Stainmore Methodists met for many years at Lane House, the home of the Croft family, near the Punch Bowl. In 1868 the North Stainmore Primitive

South Stainmore School during the Revd. Lax trial. From left to right: Mr Braithwaite, the reporter who was covering the case and who also ran a stationery shop in Kirkby Stephen; Herr Ritzema the school teacher; the Attendance Officer who checked that the children did not play truant and the Policeman from Brough. Photograph by kind permission of Mr Atkinson of Murton.

The four local young men who took part in the attack on Revd. Lax and opposite the stile where it took place.

ATTACK ON REV. J.C.LAX.M.A. VICAR OF STAIN...

Revd. Lax and Miss Mary Rennison at the court appearance in Appleby.

Methodist Chapel was built, again by public subscription. Mr A T Bird, a grocer from Brough, preached for many years at this Chapel. He held one particular record which would take some beating. He conducted the Sunday School Anniversary service for 49 years without a break.

The most infamous religious man of Stainmore, the Revd. Lax, became Vicar at St Stephen's in 1903. He was a married man, but had no children. A young school mistress at Stainmore School, Mary Rennison, caught his eye and they took to walking out together. Children from the school acted as messengers carrying notes across the field between Vicarage and

In 1913 the church was refurbished by Revd. Thomas Westgarth, in oak with seating for 100, and an east stained glass window, above the altar, was installed in memory of G. W. Dalston-Ewbanke, of Borrenthwaite - the window was given by his wife in his memory. The renovations cost, in total, almost £300 and much of the money was raised by subscription. Mr Reynoldson, Brough, was the contractor for the general masonry work and the carving of the tracery work for the east window was done by Mr G Dinwoodie. The plain plaster ceiling was replaced with an oak cornice and ornamentation panelled with oak moulding. The re-opening ceremony in 1913 is pictured opposite.

In the church doorway is Maggie Cooper of Borren House and an unknown lady; Dr and Mrs Abercrombie from Augill Castle are nearing the door. Mrs Breeks junior and Mrs Breeks senior, wife of General Breeks of Helbeck Hall, stand near the gate; Norah Bowron from Mouthlock, and Jenny Coulthard from the Vicarage, are towards the right of the picture; the men with their backs to the camera are Albert Walton of Mouthlock and Joe Walker of Swinstone. Photograph by kind permission of Mrs Pickersgill.

RE OPENING OF PARISH CHURCH. STAINMORE.

Above the new altar window, pews, ceiling and gas lamps, fitted in 1913.

School. Mary moved into lodgings, first at Borren House and later at Little Skirrigill, near Rampson, her father had been Station Master at Barras but her parents had moved to Darlington.

Local disapproval of the affair grew. People stopped going to Church and eventually plotted against the Vicar and his mistress. One night as the pair walked, up near Seats, they were waylaid by a group of young Stainmore men. After a tussle the Vicar was tied to a five-bar gate and carried down to the Vicarage, where a crowd had gathered.

The Methodist Minister read some extracts of the Bible and then the ropes were loosened and the crowd dispersed. There was no tarring and feathering as some later stories recount. The kidnappers were all fined £5 apiece at Appleby Assizes. The Revd. Lax eventually faced trial in the Consistory Court at York and was defrocked. Mary was taken to Darlington and, said Henry Dixon, "The bobbies came for Miss Rennison at t'finish. They took her away but she made a gay carry on afore they got her away. She broke all t'windows out of t'Vicarage."

After the defrocking of the Revd. Lax he left Stainmore forever and emigrated to Australia. He left a lot of patching up to be done both physically and morally. The man appointed to clear up the mess was the Revd. Thomas Westgarth from Garrigill, who could not have been a more upright man. The Church was refurbished, including the installation of a new east window dedicated to George Dalston-Ewbanke of Borrenthwaite. The Vicarage and its garden were put back in order and Revd. Thomas Westgarth became a respected and admired member of the community. He obviously appreciated his parish and took many photographs and wrote poems about the area. Some of his photographs are included in this book and his poem about Stainmore tells:

Revd. Thomas Westgarth, pictured opposite, who came to Stainmore from Garrigill in 1912. He was a much respected man and during the First World War started to farm the Church Farm himself. He was a keen amateur photographer and many of the pictures in this book are his work. Photograph by kind permission of the Revd. T. Westgarth's daughter, Mrs Pickersgill.

Of these Norwegian folks
Though long since passed away
You see the kith and kin
On Stainmore every day.

Tall men they are and fair
With strong and well knit frame
And their ways and habits
You'll find them just the same.

Firm and independent
Their necks, they still are free
And to another man
They never bow the knee.

And in their low deep tone
We hear the Northman's speech
In spite of all the schools
And what they try to teach.

The names of places too
All link us with the past
A house may tumble down
Yet will the name hold fast.

The Borrowdale Colliery on North Stainmore was the last coal mine on Stainmore to be worked and was finally closed in 1928. The area is dotted with old pits. The seams were very thin and the levels low and narrow. Both the horse, and Joss Sowerby who is riding in the tub, have tins with candles to light their way in the underground darkness. Photograph by kind permission of the Walton family.

MINING AND QUARRYING

TODAY Stainmore's fields lie undisturbed, the cows and sheep quietly munching the grass in a rural idyll. It appears to be an agricultural scene undisturbed for centuries. However, below the top soil skin lie a variety of mineral deposits. On closer inspection the landscape is covered by old wounds, scarred over by green as time has healed, where men have dug and delved for riches beneath the soil since Roman times. Poet Close describes the industrial landscape of Stainmore in the 1840s: "As these seams are narrow, the pits are numerous, and each of them marked with an immense heap of black indurated clay, taken up to give room for the hewers, a circumstance which not only blots the beauty of the countryside, but causes a considerable waste of soils."

At different times, lead, coal, barytes, even silver, have been mined in the area. Added to this every other field seems to have a small quarry where limestone has been split revealing fossils of creatures and plants hidden within for millions of years. The stone was used for building - men took it from the ground and shaped it into the houses, walls and roads of today's Stainmore. It was also used for making lime which was used as mortar and to improve the fertili-

ty of the soil. Small lime kilns are dotted around the parish and were never far from a coal pit and a limestone quarry. Poet Close writes of, "an inferior slaty coal from Slapestones which is mainly used for burning lime." One or two of the kilns operated on a larger scale, selling their finished product further afield and employing full-time limeburners. The double kiln at Barras employed two or three men and used the railway to transport the finished lime to customers in other regions.

Lead was one of the earliest substance mined from Stainmore, as it was a valuable metal, especially if it contained a high proportion of silver. The early history is somewhat foggy as there are few records, but on a map of 1828 an 'Old Smelt Mill' is marked beside Smelt Mill beck on North Stainmore. A nearby house, called Highground House is long since abandoned.

Another lead mine leased by 'George Harker, John Coat & Co., at Awgill' was blasting away beneath the ground in the 1760s. They were the biggest buyers of powder from Abraham Dent's shop in Kirkby Stephen. They were using about four pounds (just under two kilos) per week at a cost of one shilling and one penny per pound. This mine continued to be worked until the end of the nineteenth century and was a profitable and extensive operation.

In 1847 Jacob Walton prepared a report for the North Stainmore Mining Company which leased the mineral rights. There were 64 shares owned by eighteen different men, some of whom lived as far afield as Kendal.

Jacob Walton's report says that the Oregill Mine "is one of the most singular mines I have seen... the Strata all at once becomes nearly vertical." Jacob believed the seam would become, "more productive and profitable at moderate depth" and advised the owners, "to prosecute this trial with spirit and in the most effective way, and as the present engine shaft is too small for going to a great depth and is also in a bad situation... I would recommend sinking a new shaft of a much larger size in the most eligible situation... and go down about 30 fathoms and at the depth cross cut to both veins." He goes on to describe the thirty foot diameter water wheel which would be necessary to "unwater the mine."

It seems the operation was a success for a Directory of 1858 states, "At Augill... situate in a secluded and romantic vale, one and a half miles from Brough, are extensive lead mines and smelting mill, which are advantageously worked by means of machinery of a very improved and complete description." By 1860 Jacob and John Walton were both involved in the enterprise and went on to form the North Westmorland Lead Mining Company Ltd in 1880 to work the "mines and veins of lead, lead ore and barytes situated in the Manors of Brough and Stainmore." The Walton family still own the now listed Augill Smelt Mill which was curiously described on the first Ordnance Survey map of 1863 as "an iron foundry."

Gradually the lead content of these mines was worked out and barytes, found in the same veins and in the old lead spoil heaps, became more important. The Cabbish Mine near Leatherhow, previously worked for lead, was opened up for barytes. Within living memory the barytes carts would come down from Stainmore, their brakes screeching - it was extremely heavy stuff - and took some holding back. The barytes was ground to a fine powder at a mill where Brough Primary School now stands. Mrs Nicholson, late of Hillcrest, remembers, 'Dad was in the mine, and there was one or two accidents, one or two got hurt with falls of rock. I think Dad had some cracked ribs or something of the sort... it got a bit dangerous... that was during the War years... the First World War.'

The Borrowdale miners and Joss Sowerby (with the white shirt) in about 1908. The Walton family owned this coal pit, the lead mine and smelt mill at Augill. Six old pence per ton of coal raised was paid to the Lord of the Manor, Lord Hothfield, for the mineral rights. The Waltons also owned Blackmore Green and Blackmore Gate farms which were tenanted, but also grew hay for the pit ponies. All the miners are carrying walking sticks because it was a long walk to the pit face and the sticks helped them 'see' in very dark conditions. Photograph by kind permission of the Walton family, Kent and Cumbria.

The Tan Hill pits, high on the fells between Stainmore and Arkengarthdale was producing coal from an early date. The coal was at first transported by strings of pack horses. The people of Stainmore had full responsibility, in terms of cost and labour, for keeping the roads within the parish repaired. Eventually they complained because the coal traffic was ruining the roads without contributing to the repairs. A toll road was set up in the mid-eighteenth century over Stainmore to Tanhill and down into Arkengarthdale. It was one of the first in the county. Two toll gates

were set up. The gate-keeper often had another source of income as his wage was very small. Peter Thirk, gate-keeper at Molds Bar in 1813, also worked as a tailor. The collected tolls from the pack-horse trade were used to improve the road so that carts rather than packhorses could be used for transporting the coal. By kind permission of John Marsh, Photographic Archive, Kendal. The photograph above shows a miner and his pit pony coming out of the Tan Hill Pit with loaded carts of coal.

Mr Ward, born in 1900, has described how he worked at the Lunehead Mine, just outside Stainmore Parish, walking up from Brough on a Monday morning to stay for the week at the 'Shop' where Nathan Dargue was the houseman. He described conditions down this mine in the early years of this century:

Where we were conditions weren't good. In winter time we'd go in at the horse level, up about three or four ladders. In summer we'd walk up onto the fell and down the airshaft. It was good working for air, but wet... the Nacky was very wet and it wasn't really safe - you could hear the woods cracking... We bored these five or six holes in the face... we used to put the gelignite in our trouser's pockets to soften it, put it in the boreholes and put the detonators on, we always nipped them on with our teeth... stem the gelignite with clay, a bit of loose fuse and set it off, it was a contract job from Ralph Dent, a queer old lad, a grand fellar, from Stainmore. The horse had a candle in an old enamelled chamberpot and he'd hang it from the collar... There were many old workings, and they never got to the end of many of these - the Old Man had taken most of the lead out.

Tan Hill Inn, 11 miles from Kirkby Stephen, Highest Public House in England, 1732 feet. "Cat & Fiddle", Derbyshire 1690 ft. Isle of Sky, 1485 ft. "Travellers Rest", Kirkstone Pass, 1481 ft. Flask Bar, Derbyshire. 1535.

The Tan Hill Inn, showing the house in the foreground, now demolished, where many of the miners lived while working at the pits and the inn where they must have spent many hours.

Above, the Kettle Pot Coal Mine, on the summit of the Pennines. It had been worked at the end of the eighteenth and early nineteenth century and was re-opened in July 1921.

POWDER AND CANDLES

Coal mining on Stainmore started at least as early as the fourteenth century when Roger de Clifford, Lord of the Manor, received rent "for a certain mine of sea coal on Stainmore by the year 13s 4d." There always seem to have been more mines on the north side of Stainmore and many of these were being worked in the eighteenth century. An agreement of 20 January 1787 describes a typical operation. The mineral rights belonged to the Lord of the Manor, J Metcalfe Carlton.

His agent, Isaac Topping of Warehouse on Stainmore, negotiated with the collier, William Bland, to open a shaft and drive a level in Bluegrass Pasture. Isaac Topping agreed to pay five shillings per fathom of shaft or level but William, "is only to Receive one half of his Wages whatever he Earns untill ye above Bargain be finished and ye Remainder of his Wages when it is sufficiently completed." Isaac agreed to provide the woods and "Ling to Back ye Wood with." Lastly, "Wm Bland is to drive ye above Level one yard high and find a Bankman to Draw from him and find his own powder and Candles."

Two hundred years ago there wcre more than 30 men and boys employed in either getting or carrying coals on Stainmore. A typical miner's family in 1787 lived at Dummah Cragg and consisted of:

76

James Beckwith, master of family, coal miner
Mary Beckwith, wife, housekeeping
John Beckwith, son, pupil
William Beckwith, son, pupil
Ann Beckwith, daughter, knitting
Mary Beckwith, daughter, infant
Elizabeth Winter, servant, knitting etc.

In 1784 James Beckwith paid Isaac Topping, the mine agent, £74-10s-00d for renting the Loadman Colliery. He also produced a list of the tools in stock at the mine: "eleven picks, six large hammers, five Corvs, three Gablocks, two pumps, five shovels, one Bank shovel, six wedges, one pair Clotch Irons and one Coal peck." Apart from these tools each miner seems to have had, for his own use, three picks, one hammer, two wedges and a shovel. It must have been very hard work in a narrow seam with only these basic tools and a candle for light. There were fifteen miners at this colliery in 1784, but only two of them were full-time; Jonathan Birkbeck and Thomas Pearson both worked six days a week earning 8s-6d and 5s-9d respectively. The remainder of the miners were almost certainly part-time farmers and worked between one and four days a week down the pit.

The coal was sold to local farmers, but also carried to Temple Sowerby and Penrith. An eighteenth century account shows that Penrithians were paying

Coal carts waiting to collect the Borrowdale coal, circa 1910. The coal was sold at the pit head for £1 a ton and went to the local Brough and Stainmore market. When the Eden Valley railway opened Brough people started to go to Musgrave Station for coal from the North East. The Borrowdale pit continued to work, but there was little profit, and it rarely employed more than ten men. During the coal miners' strike of 1912, it was one of the only mines in the country to continue working. Photograph by kind permission of the Walton family, Kent.

Lunehead Mine showing the Top and Bottom shops, houses where the miners lodged for the working week. The woman on the left probably worked in the washing shed where barytes was cleaned and sorted - an extremely cold job in winter. Photograph by kind permission of Mrs Hinchcliffe, Murton.

1s-10d per load for Stainmore coal. The carter had eight horses which carried seven loads a week to Penrith. On 56 loads he could make £2-6s-2d a week profit. The carter's weekly costs included buying the coal at 3d a load, hay, corn, shoeing, wages, Temple Sowerby toll gate (8d) and David Kirk's gate (4s) plus, "one day's expenses at Penrith, Hay and all included 6s-10d." Windmore and Borrowdale Collieries were being worked at this date and the latter continued to operate into the twentieth century.

There are various accounts of miners being killed in the mines, usually by rock falls. However the level of operation was small scale and disasters if any, were also small scale. In March 1870 a tragedy was averted by a quick thinking boy. He had been down the Borrowdale Pit with Mr Thomas Walton of Brough and Michael Steel, a collier. They were leaving the mine when a great rush of water came towards them along the level. The boy was in front and the men shouted for him to get out and get help. The men were forced back by the water which filled the mine to the roof for a length of 60 fathoms. The miners at the surface began desperate attempts to save the two trapped men and the boy, soaked to the skin, was sent home to get dry clothes. On his way he had to cross a stream. When he got to it, it was so swollen with water that he decided to go to a bridge further down.

On his way he saw to his surprise that the stream suddenly disappeared down an old pit shaft. He ran back to raise the alarm and the other miners then diverted the stream. It took 36 hours for the water in the mine to subside so that Thomas Walton and Michael Steel could be rescued from a ledge inches above the water where they had perched for a day and half in complete darkness and with no food. They were very weak but happily recovered from the ordeal.

Frank and Harry Walton's father worked in the mine during the 1920s. By this time Borrowdale Pit was coming to the end of its life. Harry Walton recalled that his father earned 25 shillings a week and that the, "coal was so small it was only used to go for the Barytes mines - for drying it out." In the last days of the pit, "all the miners were old men." The conditions were poor and only the strikes of 1912 and 1926 brought the pit a new lease of life. Local people had taken to buying coal from Musgrave Station.

During the 1912 strike an intrepid *Cumberland and Westmorland Herald* reporter entered the mine and his account gives a clear picture of working conditions:

Donning an old torn jacket, and with an old sack to sit on, I mounted an empty tub, and off we started on our half mile ride into the bowels of the earth. Armed with two inches of candle stuck in a bit of

79

clay, and preceded by the driver on the first tub, off we started. In a minute it was stone dark, except for the faint glimmer of our two candles, and a moment afterwards I lost mine over the edge of the tub. The low roof came down so dangerously that I had to duck my head, and the working was so narrow that I more than once struck the sides with my elbows. A rather unusual rattle and a bang, and our driver pulled up stating that we were off the road. Squeezing myself against the rocky side of the track I stood clear of the tub, and it was lifted on to the rails again, and off we started... On we plodded in the darkness, and presently a faint light ahead and the murmur of voices showed that we were reaching the miners.

Eight candles lighted, eight fellows seated on a plank eating their lunch. Lunch over they wended their way to the cross workings, small burrows not more than two feet six inches high. At the very end of the main level they were excavating rock and shale, carrying it into the exhausted workings.

This unwanted material was used to hold the roof up where the men had finished working. Harry Walton recalls the end of the mine in 1928. It had been taken over by a company who plundered it in the 1926 strike and didn't follow the old maintenance procedures.

He said, "There was another older level, parallel to it and it was to walk once a year to clear soil and stones that had fallen to make an airway... a big fire near the entrance drew the air right round and a bog door covered with mats sealed it off," thereby drawing fresh air to the far workings through the old level.

"In the latter years it was never walked properly to get it clear... there was no trouble with gas when the fresh air was circulating, but when the Glover lads came to take the rails out they never got to the far end because there was no air. Gillbank Pit was finished, not by lack of air, but because it became flooded in the early years of this century."

END OF AN ERA

Apart from these 'proper' mines, there were many small workings on Stainmore, especially where coal outcropped on the surface. Mr Atkinson remembers accompanying his father to the 'mine':

We used to get coal from Kettlepot... he used to mine it himself. It was an old river bottom down in a gill... there was the beck running down this gill... and it would take him probably a week to clean this hole out.

When it came a flood it would fill this hole up with stones and all sorts of rubbish, then he'd start and get coals... and by it was a good coal... we used

This photograph, taken in the early 1930s, shows Durham miners outside the Slip Inn. The miners brought coal during the Depression from the Durham coalfields to sell in Westmorland, a cartload cost 12s-6d. These were desperate measures to find money to feed the miners and their families. William Pounder on the far right was the licensee and is providing refreshments for the thirsty miners. Photograph by kind permission of Colin Alderson.

to carry it out of this gill bottom up onto a flat place, on the top, which was maybe 20 yards and just dump it in a heap... then load it onto a horse and cart... It was a nice journey down from Kettlepot to Tufton Lodge, down through Ewbank Park.

By the 1930s there was little quarrying of stone or lime burning, and there was no lead or coal mining and even the barytes trade had come upon hard times and men had been laid off. There can be no better tribute to the end of this era, and the 'Old Man' - the Stainmore miners of long ago - than J. W. Bousfield's poem composed in 1908, two years before he left Blackmoor Green to emigrate to Australia:

> *January it was the 23rd*
> *In patches lay the snow*
> *It came a shower now and then*
> *A gentle breeze did blow.*
>
> *Eight miners they set out from Brough*
> *Ne'er dreamt what was in store*
> *For when they got to Lunehead mines*
> *Their notice got to go.*
>
> *For up spoke Billy Parkin*
> *His voice was sad and low*
> *The barytes trade's not doing well*
> *There's eight men got to go.*

> *It grieves me sore to part with you*
> *For you have served me true*
> *I never slept a wink last night*
> *My thoughts were all of you.*
>
> *And as he came to Abra'm Dent*
> *A tear stood in his eye*
> *I'm afraid poor Abe will have to part*
> *And Abra'm heaved a sigh.*
>
> *Next he came to Johnty Yare*
> *By trade a joiner he,*
> *A nagging wife to plague his life*
> *Said he, "I'll go on't spree."*
>
> *Next he spoke to Billy Chamley*
> *Just newly wed was he*
> *Said he if I had known before*
> *Ne'er married would I be.*
>
> *He seemed to take it badly*
> *And said now this is rough*
> *But I'll go home to Amy*
> *And hawk tea cakes in Brough.*
>
> *Next came Tommy Chapman*
> *Who's keen on lifting weights*
> *And talks about the girls he squeezed*
> *And other big exploits!*
>
> *Then he thought about his girl*
> *A bonny Grasmere lass*

He said he would have wed the girl
If he only had the brass.

Up spoke Peter Fawcett
He took it like a man
Said he, "I'll take the turnpike road
And tote the padding can."

Up spoke Tommy Beadle
Dufton's grand old man
"I'm far too old for heavy work
But I'll do the best I can."

"I'll try and get another job
And if I fail to do
I'll ask for the Old Age Pension
As I'm close on seventy two.

Next came Thomas Dobinson
Who farmed at Gullom Holme
He said his way he could not pay
Through farming on his own.

But up spoke poor old Tom
I'll either sink or swim
"My wife can go out washing
And I'll mind little Jim."

And next came John Rudd, Dufton
A man of sober habits
Milling was one of these
The other catching rabbits.

No more there'll be tanthundering
All up yon West End drift
For by the ikey moses,
Poor John Rudd's got the drift.

Their voices we will miss them
There's Abe's familiar ring
Beadle with his step dance
And John't the Tamborine.

There's Chapman gone on football
He always banks on Brough
And Peter puts the 'fluence on
When Dobinson starts to cough.

There's John Rudd we will miss him
We'll sit and mope and mope
He plagued us with his whistling winds
And his songs about the Pope.

I hope you'll all agree with me
Before I bid adieu
We hope and trust they all get work
And earn good money too.

And now my lay is ended
We'll join in this refrain
Are we to part like this Bill
Till the Barytes blooms again?

J. W. Bousfield, 1908.

Oxenthwaite House in 1910 was the home of Mr Harrison, a Manchester businessman. Mr Harrison was keen on shooting and a gamekeeper was employed part-time to look after the estate. The gamekeeper also worked at the Cabbish mine on North Stainmore, mining for barytes and was the author's great-grandfather. From left to right, the maid (unknown); Eleanor Davidson (née Gasgarth); Robert Davidson, the gamekeeper; Maisie Davidson; Mr Harrison; James Davidson and Miss Kate Harrison.

Boon Days and Fiddles

LIFE on Stainmore was not all hard work, but like everything else, entertainment was mostly home-made. It followed the pattern of the seasons and the work to be done on the farm. The Martinmas and Michaelmas Hiring days where indoor and outdoor servants were engaged for six months at a time were excuses for a get together, and a few days' holiday making for the servants. Sales and ancient fairs, like Brough Hill, drew the crowds together for every type of spectacle; in days long gone these included bull-baiting and cock fighting. Agricultural shows became popular in the 19th century and Stainmore held its first show at Mouthlock.

Hunting was a popular sport for the gentry, whether for grouse, deer or foxes. Poet Close, writing in 1842, mentions the good hunting on Stainmore. This lordly sport did not please all the local farmers who complained of walls and fences being damaged. But, says the notorious bard, the gentleman hunter simply replied, "Oh, it serves you right, you are fit for nothing else but to toil and dig for our pleasure; what else were you made for, I should like to learn? You can know nothing of the amusements of gentlemen! Keep your place and be thankful you are not punished for insulting men of our dignity." The Stainmore farmer's bottled up angry reply probably came thundering out at some poor sheep!

Gamekeepers were employed to look after the moors. Mr Atkinson's father came to Tufton Lodge in 1896 to work as a gamekeeper for Lord Hothfield. His son, Henry Atkinson said, "Until the First World War he got £1 a week and it went up to 30s during the War." As well as this, "he had a few sheep, a few cattle and a horse on thirteen acres. I've also known us have seventeen dogs."

As a boy Mr Atkinson used to help his father and, "from about ten-year-old we'd go on the fell regular." One of the main jobs was to keep down pests, especially crows. "We used to shoot them... he used to take one of us because carrion crows are very clever birds but they can't count... two on you go and then one walk away and the birds came back again."

Just within living memory farmers on Stainmore had 'boon' days, when neighbours gathered on one man's farm to help with hay or clipping sheep. At the end of the day a boon supper would be provided to feed the helpers, who would all move on to another

During the nineteenth century, Stainmore had become a popular place for shooting parties. This hut at the end of the Belah Viaduct was used as a shooting box. The men and boys are packing grouse from the shoot into boxes to be carried away on horseback. The shed later became a hen house at New Hall. The photograph was taken in about 1920 and is by kind permission of Mr Atkinson, Murton.

Brough's main street in the early years of the twentieth century, with the new clock tower incorporating part of the old market cross. Brough-under-Stainmore, as it was called from early times, was the main town for the people of Stainmore, providing all the necessaries of life, from shoes to pans, soap to nails. Photograph by kind permission of the Walton family, Kent and Cumbria.

Stainmore farmers might have bought some of these Scottish cattle which were for sale at Brough Hill Fair. The cattle were over-wintered in Westmorland before being sold on as beef. The drovers standing in the background walked the cattle all the way from the Scottish farms for sale at Brough Hill. Photograph by kind permission of the Walton family, Kent and Cumbria. The images opposite are of Brough Hill Fair before the First World War. Although not on Stainmore this was a highlight of the year and a popular place for local people to meet.

man's farm the next day.

The school, chapel and church were meeting places and dances and concerts were popular. Mrs Pickersgill, who lived at the Vicarage at the time, remembers:

In 1912, it was a leap year, and there was a concert given... they had a Lady Chairman, Constance Annie Ewbanke, Sis as she was known, she was the chairman of the concert, and I can remember, she was very dark and very pretty - I thought she was beautiful. She was dressed in a long green dress and at her waist she had a bunch of fresh snowdrops.

Bobby and Annie James lived at Belah Cottages near the end of the viaduct. Their father was a plate-layer on the railway. Most people on Stainmore kept livestock, whether farmers or not. There was a great deal of interest in showing poultry, sheep, cattle and produce at local shows. Photograph by kind permission of Mr Atkinson, Murton.

King Edward VII travelling through Brough, 13th October 1905.

The children of North Stainmore pictured for the May ceremony and the crowning of the May Queen.

There was plenty for the young people to do, as Mr Bainbridge, late of West Dowgill recalls:

In our younger days, before we were married, a few young people would go from one place to another, to different families, and they used to welcome us, and it used to be a sing-song round the piano - that was the main sort of social life... they used to have dances, concerts and such as that, and most of them were in the school... and the carnivals and shows were local gatherings with a lot of interest... many a time in these country places, the ladies went along to a neighbour's house to do quilting. Fellers played dominoes, or cards, and it was all chat.

Dances were held upstairs at the Slip Inn, where numbered plank walls were taken down to make a large dance floor. A piano or a fiddle player was all that was needed to start a merry night.

The Coronation celebrations of 1911 on South Stainmore with Brough Brass Band

This track is the A66 with Pennistone, Blue Bell and Street House in the background. The procession is believed to be for the Coronation of King George V in 1911. Photograph by kind permission of Mr and Mrs Bell, formerly of Thringill.

The stone laying ceremony for the new Brough Clock Tower built for the Coronation of George V in 1911. The top of the clock tower is made up of part of the old Market Cross. Mr George Dinwoodie was in charge of the construction of the clock tower and was the first official clock winder until he retired in 1926. In those days the wages were £1 a year, a gift from the late Mr Watson E Sayer.

In winter when darkness closed in quickly, and the farming day was shorter, the evenings were long and cold. It wasn't a time for idleness though, and Harry Atkinson, one of twelve children of Henry and Jane Atkinson of Tufton Lodge, remembers his mother being busy. "She was a good knitter... just like a machine, clatter, clatter, clatter, never looked to see what she was doing... You weren't to tell to go to bed. You'd probably be sitting reading the newspaper, eight o'clock would strike... she would just turn around, pull her glasses down and look at us, and everybody would disappear."

On other nights the children would help make rugs. "Sitting at home by the fire, prodding hearth rugs by candlelight, I'm an expert at that... we never used to go out anywhere... I once remember going to a concert at school and once remember going to Kirkby Stephen to a circus, that's the only time I remember going out anywhere, except maybe down to New Hall for some milk."

Dr Bainbridge of Brough who looked after many of the people of Stainmore as well as Brough and the upper Eden Valley.

ANCIENT TRADITIONS

Children made their own fun with complicated games which required the simplest equipment - stones, marbles, a rope, stick or ball. Mr Atkinson and his brothers and sisters, "used to sledge on a ladder, or a sheet of zinc. One day Jackie Walton, the postman, he said he could see there was something going down t'field, but he couldn't mek out what it was. The zinc was cutting the snow up; we saw nothing till we hit the wall at the bottom of t'field..."

In the 1840s Poet Close writes as if an ancient tradition of neighbours making the long winter evenings shorter by sharing company, the warmth of a fire and the light of a lantern was disappearing even then. He writes:

Ganging a rocking, or going with rock and spindle to the neighbour's house was a favourite pastime among our grandmothers, who had not the most distant idea of the more elegant employment of tea-drinking, and talking scandal, which has now entirely superseded spinning and knitting.

The tradition of evening visiting among neighbours lasted into the twentieth century, although the spinning and knitting of stockings certainly disappeared. It wasn't tea-drinking and scandal which stopped the old ways - they probably went very well with quilting, knitting, rug-making, dominoes and cards. The real changes have come from the invention of radio, television and the internet, alongside the car and electricity, which opened the window on an unimagined world bringing entertainment at the touch of a button inside even the most isolated home.

A Westmorland Education

THE first real chance of an education for an ordinary Stainmore child began over 400 years ago. As so often happened in rural areas, the first school was endowed by a local man who had made good in the city. In Stainmore's case, a boy called Cuthbert Buckle who was educated at 'Burwens' (Borren House) on Stainmore, went to London to make his fortune. He became a wealthy vintner and Lord Mayor of London in 1594. His will directed that a school should be built close to 'Burwens' and he gave £8 a year out of the Spital Estate to pay a schoolmaster. The inhabitants built the school house and it was dedicated, "for ye Performance of Divine Service and ye Education of Children in Religion and Good Manners."

In 1608 the school was consecrated so that it could also be used as a chapel. By the end of the century it had fallen into disrepair so in 1699 Thomas, Earl of Thanet repaired the church and school. At the same time he enclosed Slapestones, a piece of waste ground, in order to supplement the wages of the curate and schoolmaster. Another gift to the school came from the Revd. Bracken of Stainmore who died in 1754. In his will he left £5 to be invested and the interest to be given to the poor of Stainmore, "regard being had to those who have been most constant at prayers and sacraments" and, "to poor children at Stainmore School, whose parents live by hard labour, I give £5 to buy books with."

Not every child benefited from the South Stainmore Free Grammar School as it was known. In a census of 1787 there are 43 pupils listed - all of them boys! The girls of school age were at home knitting stockings and some of the boys were working on farms or in the mines. Forty three boys must have been a handful and the Revd. John Mason Fenton, curate and schoolmaster, needed some help. Jonathan Ewbanke was the assistant schoolmaster. He bought some of his books from Abraham Dent's shop in Kirkby Stephen. They included copies of Virgil, Terence, Ovid and Horace - a Stainmore education included the classics.

The Revd. Fenton lived with his widowed mother, Elizabeth, and his sister Nancy, who was housekeeper and a seamstress. The Fentons only had one servant - Isabel Brunskill. She wasn't a house maid however, as her job was described as 'husbandry' - in today's language she was a farm labourer.

North Stainmore School in 1905. The school was opened in 1880 and closed in 1959. North Stainmore previously had a school up the road towards Long Crag - it is mentioned as early as 1812, but this building has now disappeared. Photograph by kind permission of Mrs Buckle, Brough.

South Stainmore School in 1907. On the far left is Miss Rennison, the school teacher involved in the Revd. Lax affair; and on the far right is Herr Ritzema. The children are dressed in their Sunday best for the photographer's visit. Photograph by kind permission of Mr Colin Alderson, Alnwick.

North Stainmore School in 1937. The school had 50 children in 1905 and two teachers. The numbers had dwindled by 1937 to the twelve on this photograph. On the back row, left to right, are Alice Swinbank, the teacher; Margaret Clark; George Dent; Frank Bailes, who was killed while working in the Helbeck Quarry in 1939; Laurie Robson and Lily Clark. Middle row: Jean Pratt; Betty Coates; Arthur Sowerby; Mabel Dent and George Bailes. In the front are Trevor Dent and John Coates. Photograph by kind permission of Mr T. Dent.

Education was seen as important because Stainmore farms were generally small and would not be economic if divided for inheritance. Daughters would be maid servants and then marry, sons had to be set up in the world. If they couldn't inherit the farm, an education would help them in another trade or profession. A Westmorland education in the 1830s, said Lord Brougham and Vaux was "the best in England, even as good as the best Swiss schools." This didn't mean however, that everyone could read and write. The Stainmore marriage registers show that many people, especially women, couldn't sign their own names.

A school was established on North Stainmore during the eighteenth century, but it doesn't appear to have been in continuous use. Sometimes it's called 'The Old School' and sometimes 'The School House.' Part of the school was a cottage for the school master or mistress and later it became two miners' cottages. The old North Stainmore school was near Long Cragg.

After the 1870 Education Act, education was compulsory and School Boards were set up. The South Stainmore Board used the former Grammar School building adjacent to the church and the North Stainmore Board built a new school which was opened in August 1880. Within living memory there were 50 and 60 pupils at both schools. Mrs

Nicholson, late of Hillcrest (previously known as Street House), remembers her school days before the First World War:

I went to South Stainmore School until I was nine-year-old and there was a German teacher, Mr Ritzema, I used to like him, but a lot of people didn't like him, ...I felt I could learn from him, in fact he wanted to persuade Mother to let me lodge over there, he could make a scholar of me, but Mother didn't want me to, she wanted me with her.

All the children would walk to school, summer and winter, from the isolated farms and houses of Stainmore. Mr Atkinson, who lived at Tufton Lodge as a boy, proved that the schoolchildren of yesterday were made of tough stuff. He explained:

Getting the groceries once per month... Mother would run out of something and she'd say, "When you come out of school tonight, pop down to Brough and get so and so." So we'd walk three mile to school, another three miles down to Brough, five mile back to Tufton Lodge, before you got your tea and after you'd had your tea, she'd say, "You can go to the Station and post these letters now."

South Stainmore School in 1938. Top row, left to right: Dennis Walton; ? Bainbridge; Dick Mounsey; Ken Guy; ? Bainbridge; John Davis. Second row: Cathy Bainbridge; Elva Walton; William Wearmouth; Jim Davis. Third row: ? Bousfield; Hilda Richardson; Grace Hunter; Irene Hunter; Dorothy Guy; Gladys Brogden; Laura Thompson; ? Thompson; Ella Pratt; Vera Walton; Margaret Guy; Monica Guy. Front row: Jimmy Guy; Lewis Richardson; Geoff Atkinson; Ronnie Bousfield; Derek Buckle; John Guy; Lesley Ingham; Ronald Alderson; Jimmy Richardson and ? Bainbridge. Photograph by kind permission of Mr C. Alderson.

Miss Thompson who was the teacher at North Stainmore School.

Two busy thriving schools with 50 or 60 pupils each were only fifty years later facing closure. North Stainmore was closed first, in 1959, and was turned into a village hall. South Stainmore remained open until 1970, when only five pupils were left. Three of the children had the same surname - Pauline, Kevin and Wilfred Buckle. It is a sad irony that 400 years after Cuthbert Buckle's endowment, three of the last children to benefit from a Stainmore education shared his surname.

THE PLAINS OF HEAVEN

STAINMORE has gained a reputation, particularly amongst lowland dwellers and travellers, based upon the winter weather broadcasts. The A66 is one of the first cross-Pennine routes to block with snow and has always commanded respect from travellers, whether in summer or winter. In days gone by the boggy ground, the muddy ruts of the road jolting horse-drawn carriages, the fog and snow quick to blow up and blot out vision, must have made this a fearful place, where an unwary traveller could meet his Maker. Unfortunately many still do meet their Makers on the A66.

The other aspect of this ancient route which commands respect is the stupendous view across the dappled green patterns of the Eden Valley to the Lake District and Howgill fells. The scene hasn't changed for centuries and yet is never the same. The seasons, weather, the patterns of cloud and light repaint the picture by the hour. The view is known as 'The Plains of Heaven.'

One of the first tourists to Stainmore, Sir Daniel Fleming, wasn't inspired by the scenery however. He was far more concerned about the discomforts of travelling this former Bronze Age trade route and Roman road. He wrote in 1671:

here beginneth to rise that high, hilly, and solitary country, exposed to wind and rain, which, because it is stony is called in our native language Stane-Moor; over which is a great (but no good) road, the post passing twice every week betwixt Burgh and Bowes, and coaches going often that way, though with some difficulty and hazard of overturning and breaking. All here round about is nothing but a wild desert, unless it be an homely hostelry or inn, in the midst thereof, called the Spittle on Stainmore, for to entertain wayfaring people.

The Spittle was recorded as early as 1171 when it was a 'hospital' or hostel erected by the Abbey of Merrick to accommodate travellers, later becoming an inn. It would have been a welcome sight to travellers, most of whom would cross Stainmore on foot. In earlier years the road did not necessarily follow the same course and guides could be hired to take travellers across the moor. One of them, Joseph Horn, is recorded to have been blind! During the eighteenth century, whether blind or sighted, the journey from

Windmore End, North Stainmore, home of the Dent family for many years. The Dents came from Grains o' the Beck, near Middleton. In the yard there is a sledge which was the usual conveyance for hay and other goods on the farm. Until the days of the tractor, few upland farmers had carts or trailers as the sledge and a horse travelled much better over bumpy roads, snowy or muddy fields, and, being low, it was easier for one man to load. Photograph by kind permission of Mr Trevor Dent, Brough.

Brough to Bowes took at least six hours.

The Stainmore becks proved a difficulty for travellers and local people alike. The turbulent waters of the Belah flowing through a deep, thickly wooded, and rocky gill, cut Stainmore off from Kirkby Stephen. In 1576 Sir Cuthbert Buckle, Lord Mayor of London, remembered the home and people of his youth by building a bridge over Belah at Oxenthwaite. It is still known as Buckle's Bridge.

The roads at this time were bridlepaths and the only form of transport which could cope with the rough mountain terrain were pack-horses. They carried everything from wool to wheat and on South Stainmore strings of them would come down from Tan Hill every day, laden with coal. The pack-horse trade added plenty of wear and tear to the tracks but did not contribute to the maintenance. The upkeep of the roads was paid for, usually in labour, by the parish. On 8 January 1683 the parishioners had had enough and, "upon the petition of the tenants and neighbours on the south side of Stainmoordale, it is ordered that all those that make benefit by carrying coals to pay 2d toll for every horse, for and towards the repair of the way to the coalpits."

Toll roads by bringing in revenue from their main users, took the burden off the parish, gradually allowing better roads to be built. Road mending became the job of paid workers, instead of a grudgingly undertaken duty of every member of the community. It was hard and poorly paid work - breaking stones all day and filling the ruts. Beneath Mouthlock Chapel, "an old man used to live by himself in the far end cottage. He used to work on the road and he used to take an alarm clock in a basket to work to tell the time."

By 1842 Poet Close writes, "the road to the Tan-Hill coal-pits, which a few years ago, was only a bridle-path up the valley by the side of a brook" has now gone. Instead "on the margin, where the soil was firm and secure, there the road was made. Now instead of strings of horses, ponys and asses, with back-loads of coals, may be seen scores of carts, waggons etc., thundering along the road, the echo sounding from one end of the county to the other." What would Poet Close have made of the railway's steam engines which would soon be puffing across Stainmore, or today's A66 traffic?

THE CARRIERS

Despite the improvements to the main through roads, most Stainmore houses still only had rough tracks with many gates to open. The horse and sled was often better suited to the terrain than the cart. Henry Dixon in the winter of 1947 lived at Borrowdale Beck and, "used to sled the milk t'Punch Bowl, straight over the wall tops with a horse; I'd mebbe fetch for two or three farmers around."

A cloudburst in 1931 caused havoc. Fred Alderson, standing in the river which suddenly engulfed the A66, is trying to persuade a reluctant car driver to leave his car before it gets washed over the edge. Photograph by kind permission of Trevor Dent, Brough.

Mr Dalston-Ewbanke's snow bound car on the A66 near Palliard in 1936 - a sight not unfamiliar with travellers today. Photograph by kind permission of Mr Atkinson, Murton.

By the mid-nineteenth century a complicated network of carriers had developed. In 1858 for instance there was, "Thomas Raine from his house at Rampson, to Kirkby Stephen on Mondays and to Barnard Castle on Wednesdays. James Brunskill from Upmanhow, the same. Benjamin Blackett, from Skerrygill, the same... John Thompson, from 'Black Horse,' Slip Inn, to Applebys on Saturday, Barnard Castle Wednesday and Kirkby Stephen Mondays. James Holiday from 'Greyhound,' Slip Inn (the same towns)."

Groceries were delivered once a month by cart from shops in Brough or Kirkby Stephen. Mrs Nicholson remembers that, "Hiltons of Brough used to have a chap called A. T. Bird; he used to come round for your orders, and we'd get them once a month... and there was Hastwells of Kirkby Stephen... At one time there was five going round for orders."

The reign of the horse had continued despite the arrival of railways, but it could never compete with cars and motorcycles which came to Stainmore at the turn of the century. One of the first must have been King George V in his 40 horse power Mercedes. He set out in 1905 on a journey from Brougham Hall to Raby Castle. The whole 40 mile stretch of road had been swept by hand so the King's car would not be jolted by a loose stone. On his return he was so impressed by 'The Plains of Heaven' view, that he stopped his car to watch the sun set over the Lake District.

Other tourists arrived, including the charabancs of sight-seers and holiday makers. Mrs Nicholson remembers that, "Charoloads would come to the Punch Bowl, and my mother would sometimes go to help Mrs Spooner, and oh dear, it was awful to see those poor women perspiring, standing over the stove."

Despite improved vehicles and roads, the Pennine weather still claimed its victims as it had always done. In 1931, for instance, a storm caused a flash flood, tiny streams turning to raging torrents. Mrs Nicholson told the story of an early motorist. "There was a flood just down from the Punch Bowl where the bridge is and Fred Alderson said, 'This daft feller he wouldn't get out of the car, he was wanting to go right through.' He hadn't sense, you know, that he couldn't possibly get through."

The unsuspecting traveller can soon meet more than he bargained for with Stainmore weather when even the farmers and shepherds are sometimes caught out. Henry Dixon remembers:

We had a neighbour lost one night, least we thought he was lost. We knew he was at t'fell and it was a bad night and I was milking. We had a

Steam engine number 76018 snowbound on the Stainmore line.

servant lad I believe then, we used to hire a lad until our Molly got up a bit and Bob Clarke, next farm to me, landed, he says:

'A want thee to gan with me. Eddie Bell's nivver come back from t'fell.' It was gaan on, I should think it was mebbe 7 o'clock, we hadn't finished neither so I says, 'If I's gaan t'fell I want sommet to eat wid me, you'll ha' to wait till Mrs puts me summat to eat up.' Cos you were naa good up there if thas hungry you know... There was Bob Clarke, Ernie Thompson, Jimmy Thompson and Fred... five or six on us went, and we met him coming. Aye, it's a good job we did...

The Plains of Heaven could come close to Hell as S. Alderson of Stainmore tells in *A Tragedy of the Fells.* Three young men from Grains o'Beck set out to gather sheep on the fell in October 1891. A 'tempest wild' blew up and before they could get home young John Dent was dead. His brother, Joseph, and cousin Joseph Bowman Dent got safely back. Others were not so lucky as many entries in the parish registers record, for example: "Wm Whelpdale, Borrowdale, John Moor and John Lamb of Brough Sowerby, perished by the inclemency of the weather on Saturday 25th January 1794."

The boundary stone set against the west parapet of Blackhause Bottom Bridge. It is about three feet high with angled sides, but somewhat damaged by being hit by a vehicle. It is inscribed: 'Township of South Stainmore' on the south side and 'Township of Middle Stainmore' on the north side.

BUILDINGS OF STAINMORE

THERE are very few remains above ground of early Stainmore buildings. Maiden Castle still survives from the Roman period, but De Ewbank's twelfth century fortress on Stainmore has long since disappeared. Some of Stainmore's present day houses appear to have been built on sites occupied for many centuries, perhaps even as far back as their Viking names suggest.

In the fifteenth century, on the death of John de Clifford, an inquisition shows that he owned eleven 'messuages called vaccaries' near Brough - these were tenanted parcels of land with dwellings, and a *vaccary* was a cow farm.

The ones on Stainmore were: 'Knolhow, Skrythergill, Calfhowelade, Ald Park, Swynstywath, Mouthowlake, Thornehowegayll, Burghway, Severyg, Strykescales, Hegerscale and one park called the Old Park, worth in the whole by the year £10-10s-10d.' These medieval dwellings mostly still exist, although their fabric has been worked into later houses.

A - Hearth
B - Spice cuphoard
C - Inglenook window
D - Heck partition
E - Mullion window
F - Oak beam
G - Kitchen
H - Dairy/pantry
I - Stone staircase
J - Timber loft partition
K - Sleeping space with oak plank floors
L - Single light unglazed windows

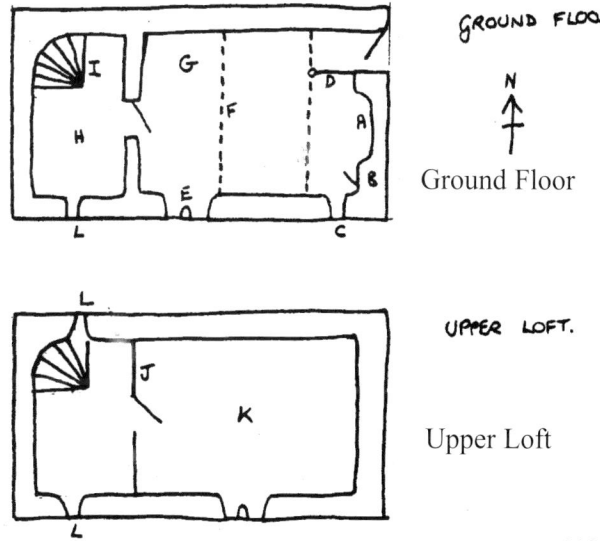

Ground Floor

Upper Loft

Borren House, photographed in 1912 - little has changed since this photograph was taken. At this time the farm belonged to the Ewbankes of Borrenthwaite and Mr and Mrs Cooper and their three children were tenants. The dairy produce was renowned - Mrs Cooper sold eggs, butter, cream and cheese. The cream was so thick it had to be spooned out and the Stainmore cheese made in the back kitchen, and kept in a little cheese room upstairs, took weeks to make. Photograph by kind permission of Mrs Pickersgill.

Great Skerrygill and Borrenthwaite Hall, in the distance, photographed in 1912. At this time Great Skerrygill was the home of the Sanderson family - Mr Sanderson, senior, Tommy, his son and Mary, his daughter. Tommy also farmed Gillses and every morning met John Dixon from Upmanhowe, both men walking to feed and water their stock. They would sit for half an hour come rain or shine and were known as 'The Daily Mail'. When Revd. Westgarth first visited the Sandersons, he was just leaving when Mr Sanderson, who had found work to do in the barn while the vicar visited, called out to his daughter, 'An' what sek a fella is he?' The author and her family have lived at Great Skerrygill since 1985. Photograph by kind permission of Mrs Pickersgill (Revd. Westgarth's daughter).

In the same order as above, Knowa was the old Vicarage, Great Skerrygill, Calvaload, Old Park, Swinstonewath, Mouthlock, Thorneygale, Broughway (unknown), Seavyrigg, Stricegill, Heggerscale and Park House (near Augill Castle).

During the seventeenth century houses on Stainmore became more substantial - many of them survive in various states of preservation. Some of them were abandoned and turned into barns during the nineteenth century recessions, for instance Calvaload and Browneshaw. Others survive as part of larger, improved houses and some were demolished. Seventeenth century Stainmore families lived in houses which were built from local materials. Almost always they were built to face the sun in a southerly direction. A typical house of 1650 would have been something like the plan (see page 113).

In earlier times windows were small single openings, or mullioned. The smaller windows were very often unglazed and presumably would be stuffed with rags if a gale was blowing. The hearth was large for burning peat or wood. The upper floor, beams, roof timbers and partitions were often made of oak. The spice cupboard for keeping precious commodities dry, including tea, salt and spices, was near the hearth. The staircase was stone and curved up in a corner of the smaller room. The sleeping lofts would be within the pitch of the roof and open to the thatch

above. There are enough surviving details of this type of house on Stainmore to allow this picture to be drawn with some accuracy.

The furniture at this time would be minimal. The will of Elizabeth Cleasby of Browneshaw who died in 1718, gives an inventory of her worldly possessions:

Her Purse and Apparell	*£1-10-00*
Shooll Lin and Hardin	*12-00*
Books and other Impliments	*5-00*
One Corn sock and one poak	*1-06*
Hardin Yarne	*9-00*
Tow Chests and tow boxes	*14-02*
One table	*1-06*
Town Unspune	*3-00*
One putter dish, Candlestick and one plate	*2-00*
One kettle and one pan	*5-06*
One Longsettle, one chare, one stoll	*2-06*
One pare of weighscailles and other Impliments	*3-00*
Owing to the Deceased by Michael Yearker	*2-00-00*
Total	*£8-07-10*

It seems that Elizabeth Cleasby was employed in weaving 'hardin' being fabric made from flax and 'lin' being linen. Her husband, died ten years earlier and his will also survives, which shows he was a soap maker with tallow, oil and potash listed in his will.

Manor House and Slip Inn photographed in the winter of 1912. During the middle part of the nineteenth century, both buildings were public houses - called the Greyhound and the Black Horse respectively. Mr and Mrs Pounder from Wensleydale kept the Slip Inn at the beginning of the twentieth century. Mrs Pounder also kept a shop in her pantry, remembered well for its stock of sweets. The pub had stone flag floors and all the cooking was done on an Althams black range. Every evening candles or hand paraffin lamps were lit for the regulars - the school teacher, and old Mr Willy Walton from Mouthlock Chapel. George Dalston-Ewbanke from Borrenthwaite slipped in occasionally too - notice the small cottage which used to stand directly opposite the Slip Inn. Photograph by kind permission of Mrs Pickersgill.

This page, two rare nineteenth century photographs of the Slip Inn. The picture right shows the inn when the landlady was Elizabeth Holliday. The image below is even older as the building has not yet been extended to the left.

Opposite, Old Park pictured in 1911. The house is first mentioned in 1670 when one Willyam Morland lived here. It was the home of the Hilton and Hopes families and was part of the Earl of Thanet's estate until 1819 when it became the

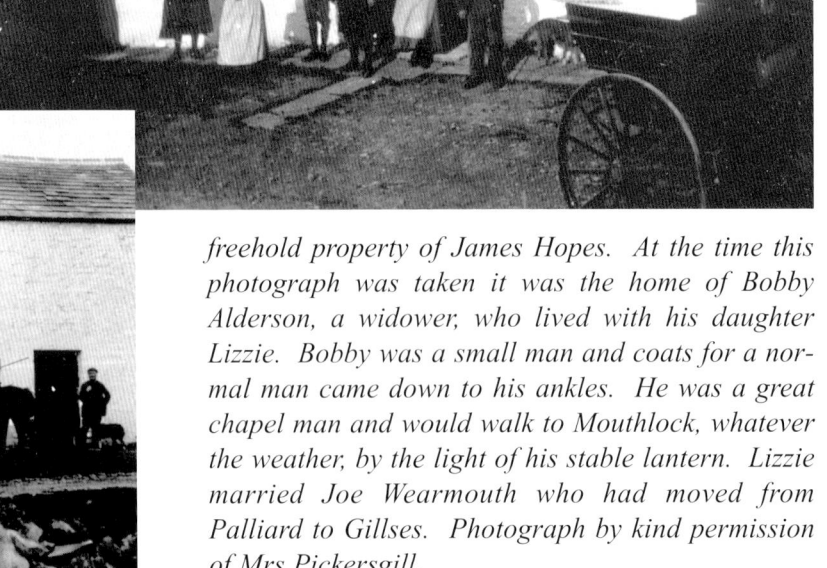

freehold property of James Hopes. At the time this photograph was taken it was the home of Bobby Alderson, a widower, who lived with his daughter Lizzie. Bobby was a small man and coats for a normal man came down to his ankles. He was a great chapel man and would walk to Mouthlock, whatever the weather, by the light of his stable lantern. Lizzie married Joe Wearmouth who had moved from Palliard to Gillses. Photograph by kind permission of Mrs Pickersgill.

The houses on Stainmore which go back to the seventeenth century if not before, include Argill, Augill Head, Barras, Blackmore Gate, Bleathgill, Bluegrass, Borren, Borrowdale, Buckles, Calva, Craco, Crag Green, Cragg House, West Dowgill, Dowgill Head, Duck Pool, Dummah Hill, Dyke House, Gillbank, Great Skerrygill, Green Cragg, Greena, Grey Lodge, High Ewbank, Inghead, Knowah, Leatherhow, Light Trees, Littlethwaite, Littsgarth, Long Cragg, Mouthlock, New Hall, Oak Bank, Old Park, Oxenthwaite, Palliard, Park Houses, Pennistone, Rampson, Seavyrigg, Little Skerrygill, Slip Inn, Stricegill, Swindale, Swinstonewath, Thorneygale, Upmanhow, Well Head, Windmore End and Woodside. There was more than one house at some of these places. For instance in 1720, Dr Hugh Todd, Vicar of Penrith, mentions the village of High Ewbank which had 20 families at that time. Added to this there were 56 scattered houses in the rest of Stainmore parish, according to Dr Todd.

Opposite, top, Upmanhowe with South Stainmore Chapel in the distance and, below, the Vicarage with, to the right, the old building which was the former vicarage a building called Knowah. Photographs by Revd. Westgarth, circa 1911, by kind permission of his daughter Mrs Ella Pickersgill.

THE AFFLUENT YEARS

The eighteenth century was a period of growing agricultural wealth, and Stainmore prospered, especially during the Napoleonic Wars. Today's landscape of walls, field houses, barns and houses was created more at this time than at any other. Field houses were built to house hay gathered from the surrounding fields; in winter these field houses also housed the stock, and the arrangement worked very conveniently.

Styles of architecture from outside began to percolate into the area for the first time, especially the Georgian style. The old houses were improved and about 30 new houses were built. The symmetrical frontage of the Georgian style, with decorated doorways and sash windows was adopted by those who could afford it. In some cases 'outshots' were built on to provide a proper staircase and extra rooms, helping to produce a fashionable four room square house. Hearths gradually became smaller as coal became the more usual fuel, and later in the nineteenth century, the 'Althams' range became a popular fixture. The former thatched roofs were replaced by more water-tight stone flags. During this process the roof would be heightened to provide full-height, ceilinged, room upstairs. This had a double function as, to keep water out a thatched roof had to be steep. A steep pitch wasn't suitable for heavy stone flags which risked sliding off the roof. A characteristic decoration was the 'kneeler,' the carved stones on the corners of the roof.

Quite a number of Stainmore's houses have at one time or another also served as inns or alehouses. Some, like the Punch Bowl and Slip Inn (called the Black Cock in 1724 and the Black Horse in the 1800s) survived into the twentieth century. The days of beer and song in public houses on Stainmore are no longer. The following were some of the old public houses: Banks House, The Bay Horse, Blackmore Green, Blue Bell, Cragmire (at Borrenthwaite), Cooper House (called New Inn), Hazelbank Inn, Leatherhow, Slapestones Inn, Manor House (called the Greyhound) and Swinging Gate.

Until the nineteenth century Stainmore parish did not have any 'grand' houses. However the Ewbank family had gradually become more wealthy than their neighbours and their homes reflected this wealth. Little Skerrygill, as it was originally called, or Skirrigill Farm, as it is now known, was improved to a high standard in the eighteenth century and then, in the nineteenth century, Borrenthwaite Hall was rebuilt around a former farmhouse to a standard of Victorian elegance.

John Bagot Pearson, "an eccentric batchelor, who came from Kirkby Lonsdale," decided that Stainmore was the perfect country retreat and built the greater part of Augill Castle on the site of a former farm-house in 1841. It is described as:

> ...an extensive Gothic building, with six massive towers. The conservatory is 40 yards long, and the opening Cloister of the same length. On the staircase is one of the most splendid windows in the North of England, designed from Melrose Abbey... The Library and its stained glass window are designed from those at Abbotsford. In this window are the armorial bearings of the Pearsons, and in the centre is St Peter, holding a key in each hand.

Previous centuries brought some improvements in housing standards through structural changes. The major advances made in the last century relied not so much on building techniques, but on pipes and wires. Borrenthwaite was the first house to be lit by electricity on Stainmore. One dry summer, just before the First World War, John Anthony Dixon of Upmanhow, built a weir across Argill Beck to divert water down a pipe to a small turbine house. The electricity created was then taken by wires held on wooden pylons across to Borrenthwaite. Since the Second World War all the houses have been connected to mains electricity supply. It provided light and power for many labour saving devices on the farm and in the home.

Augill Castle, built in 1841 for John Bagot Pearson, a business man who also lived part of the time at Kirkby Lonsdale. The castle was sold in 1906, the date of this photograph, to Mr Paul Kester, an American playwright. He bought the castle on the strength of this photograph and sent his bid by cable. Photograph by kind permission of Mr and Mrs Atkins, Brough.

Stainmore cannot be described as the sort of place which is short of water, but plentiful as the water is, it was hard work to provide it where it was needed. In previous times it had to be pulled, pumped and carried from well or spring. With pipes, taps and electric pumps it could be instantly flowing wherever it was needed, in the house or byre. Mr Bainbride said that when he first moved to West Dowgill: "there wasn't running water and no electric. The water was behind the house and it was to pull up to the house and there was a hand pump in the back kitchen, and you pumped your water... you had to pump it for t'cattle as well - I let the cattle go down there and carry their own!"

In many ways housing standards on Stainmore had not changed greatly for centuries. The houses had more room, better windows and better cooking facilities, but housework still had to be done by hard work, particularly fetching coal and water for cooking and washing; and the lavatory was still outside! The arrival of electricity and piped water allowed a revolution of comfort in the home and farmyard. As Mr Bainbridge said, "Electric was the finest thing that ever came to Stainmore."

Left, Windmore End in the snow with a cow wanting to get into the house! Photograph by kind permission of Mr Trevor Dent.

Below, Augill Head in 1930, photograph by kind permission of Mrs Badley.

Barras Station and Hotel in 1917 at which time Mr and Mrs Simpson lived there. During the grouse shooting season they had people to stay and Jim Bowron, signalman at Belah and his wife, lived round the back. There was always a roaring fire in the waiting room and it became a local entertainment to see the last train going by and sit by the fire. In the bottom left corner of this photograph is the station master's sister-in-law Lilly Calvert with Margery Simpson, the little girl on the sledge.

THE last day of August 1859 was a day of excitement, of achievement and of relief. Men laid down their tools, made their way in the warm early evening to gather upon the viaduct they had toiled and sweated to create. A few official words were spoken, and no doubt a few wry comments added. A piece of paper was rolled up and placed inside a bottle and then lowered gently into the central column of the eighth pier of the viaduct. The paper read:

"1000 feet long, 60 feet span, 200 feet high, 16 iron pillars and 2 stone buttresses. Commenced 19th July 1859, completed in 43 days:

To future ages these lines will tell
Who built this structure o'er the dell
Gilkes Wilson with these eighty men
Raised Belah's viaduct o'er the glen."

The official pat on the back over, the navvies, young men and old, set off in high spirits for their lodgings. At this time there were about 150 railway workers living on Stainmore - lodging in farmhouses and living in any empty space available.

In 1861 Mary David, widow and mother of four children, was innkeeper at the Slip Inn which was home to 44 people, 28 of them working on the railway. She must have been a woman and a half to cope with the celebrating men that night. Many of them came from far afield, some were Irish and most were unmarried. It certainly was an occasion to celebrate, as these men had built, "one of the most imposing triumphs of engineering skill in the British Isles."

The atmosphere must have sparkled with elation, success after hard work, the happiness of comradeship, music and tall stories, as the men drank and smoked their pipes in the crowded Slip. Yet beneath it all lapped a wave of unspoken sadness. They were men far from their homes and their own people. Some were young and adventurous and had been tempted by the railway's wages away from work at home. Others were older men, their adventures spent, looking back on a nomadic life following the metal rails, their life away from home having mostly cut them off from marriage and children.

Once a young man became a navvy it would be hard for him to fit back into his home town where jobs might be few and wages lower. A notice in Kirkby Stephen in 1860 offered work for '50 good

The Belah Viaduct, built in 1859, to the design of Sir Thomas Bouch by Gilkes Wilson and his men in 43 days. Sir Thomas Bouch also designed the ill-fated Tay Bridge which collapsed in high winds in December 1879 when a train was crossing over it and 75 people lost their lives. In contrast, the Belah Viaduct stood for a century and took longer to demolish in the early 1960s, than it had taken to build. A poem was placed inside the centre column of the eighth pier which read, '1000 feet long, 60 feet span, 200 feet high, 16 iron pillars and two stone buttresses. Commenced 19th July 1859, completed in 43 days. Photograph by kind permission of Mr Kirkbride, Penrith.

The Belah Viaduct carried the South Durham and Lancashire Union Railway which opened in 1861. The railway carried Durham coke to the Furness iron and steel industry in West Cumberland. It was also much used as an early tourist route, carrying visitors from the North East to the seaside at Blackpool and Morecambe. Two engines were needed to haul fully laden trains up to Stainmore Summit, a height of 1,370 feet above sea level. Photograph by kind permission of Cecil Ord.

Above an early image of the Belah Signal box. The image, above right, shows the same signal box and steam engine number 82028, a class 3 standard tank engine, which operated on the Stainmore line between 1955 and 1958 to run the passenger services between Penrith and Darlington. With thanks to Mark Keefe for the engine information.

masons' at five shillings a day, plus 200 navvies, required at 3s.1d to 3s.4d a day.

Given these ingredients, plus a local population who had been quietly minding their own business, it is not difficult to imagine that there would be trouble. The Stainmore farmers' daughters were no doubt kept securely at home whilst drunkenness, fighting and pilfering were rife. The Chief Constable of the Westmorland and Cumberland force, "recommended that four constables would be necessary" to keep order. The railway company however would only

An early photograph of railway workers in action. Photograph courtesy of the late Mr Thornborrow, Slip Inn.

pay for one. Mr Hoole writes:

His wages were £1.1s per week, plus 1s.5d a month boot allowance and 1s a month for oil. He was also allowed a great coat, cape and badge, coat, two pairs of trousers, and one hat and stock. It was agreed that his duties did not include the preservation of game, and presumably the navvies' poaching activities had to be curbed by the gamekeepers employed by the local landowners.

The navvies were labourers for progress as it marched even across such pastoral terrain as Stainmore. Wealthy businessmen saw the economic sense and the Victorian engineers prided themselves on making the impossible possible. The South Durham and Lancashire Union Railway, despite the difficulties of gradient, terrain and weather conditions, would become an artery for carrying coal and coke from County Durham to the iron works on Cumbria's west coast. The first sod was cut at Kirkby Stephen by the Duke of Cleveland on 25 August 1857. Sir Thomas Bouch was the engineer of the Belah Viaduct, and the famous Tay Bridge in Scotland, which collapsed whilst a train was crossing, killing 75 people.

The frontier days of the railway builders over, the new railway settled down to quieter times. Two special engines had been commissioned for the line - the

160 Brougham and the 161 Lowther - at £2,050 each. As they steamed up the fell, often with an engine at front and rear, to get their heavy loads up the gradient, local people soon became accustomed to the sight and sound.

Farm workers in the fields kept time by the trains and the station at Barras opened up new horizons. A 'senior citizen' writing to the *Cumberland and Westmorland Herald* said, 'Thank God we had a lifeline - the railway from Darlington to Tebay with a station at Barras from which we got our papers, coals in bulk for winter and groceries and goods of all kinds... Four to five trains ran each way daily, but nearly all required a good trudge across fields to catch them.'

The railway meant steady employment for quite a number of families - and new cottages were built to house them - two at Cragg Green and three at Summit (now demolished). Signalmen before 1914 were paid between 25s and 27s plus an extra shilling for Belah box, 'for keeping a sharp look-out for fires on the viaduct timbers' and at Summit box, 'because of the difficulty in getting men at low wages owing to the remote position of the box.' Some seemed to have enjoyed the isolation. Mr Pearson recalls:

I spent the happiest days of my life in this isolated cabin at Stainmore... To the townsman, with his

Pictured in the 1950s, engine number 43018, heading east, just after Black Hause Bridge with the old A66 road on the right. The 43018 engine was a class 4 Ivatt Mogul, otherwise known as a 'flying pig.'

A twin-engined goods train passes the railway cottages near Stainmore Summit, with the old A66 in the background. These cottages are now demolished. Photograph by kind permission of Mr J Armstrong.

limited horizon of brick walls, beer and bingo, Stainmore Summit must have seemed 'stuck out in the wilds'... Never again will an aspiring young signalman become acquainted with the beauty of a sunrise on a summer morning, the call of the grouse in the heather... or the simply breathtaking majesty of a sunset over the Eden Valley. I treasure most of all the memory of the brilliance of the Northern Lights seen during the night shifts when it did seem as if the stars could be plucked out of their velvet background, so clear did they appear. When one of the coloured searchlights of the aurora shot across the sky, things began to happen in the cabin. Bells used to jingle, block indicators danced and the phonophore telephone circuit would crackle like a demented geiger counter.

Mr Pearson saw the harsh side of Stainmore too, and remembers the winter of 1947 when the line was full of snow from sleepers to the top of bridges, 45 feet deep in some places, and as he walked he stepped over the telegraph wires. The trouble started on 3 February when a passenger train got stuck as it climbed up from Kirkby Stephen. They managed to get the passengers out to safety, but the blizzard continued to rage, burying the train. Men began digging to clear the blockage but ended up thrce miles further back than they started. Flame-throwers, jet engines mounted on trains, snowploughs, even explosives were used to try and move the hard-packed snow. Finally the only thing that proved completely reliable and effective was 'a pair of hands and a large shovel,' and the line was reopened by the end of March.

The line had its share of accidents in fact, as Mr Hoole writes, 'Perhaps more than its share when there were heavy mineral trains to be worked up and down long gradients. In the early days there were long stretches of single line and with the primitive signalling it is not surprising that accidents occurred with regrettable frequency.' Luckily most accidents did not involve loss of life. In 1867, for example, one accident involved four trains; the first, stuck in the snow, managed to warn the second in time. The third didn't quite stop in time and 'knocked a truck off the line, but did not damage it much' and the fourth train just crashed... doing a fair amount of damage to engines and trucks and blocking the line.

Mr Atkinson witnessed a near disaster at Belah, 'I remember a train running down there one night, half past eight one night. I think they were supposed to put so many brakes on up at Summit and he didn't put his brakes on and away it went with them. But they managed to get 'phoned down to Kirkby Stephen to get the railway closed... it stopped somewhere up towards Smardale.'

A photograph of Barras Station in 1913 with piles of snow on the platform. The photograph was taken by Revd. Westgarth and shows steam engine number 329 pulling passenger carriages. The locomotive is a class 901, built at Gateshead in 1876 to an Edward Fletcher design by the N.E.R. and rebuilt in 1888. Sadly, it was scrapped in 1919. With thanks to Mark Keefe for the engine details.

Barras Station in 1916. From left to right: unknown; Mrs Joe Bowron, the signalman's wife and her daughter Rosamund; Lilly Calvert, a lady porter who emigrated to Canada in 1917; Mr Simpson, the Station Master and his daughter Margery. The trains were stopped, even buried in the snow in some of the bad winters - 1933 and 1947 especially. In the blizzards of 1933 a complete train was buried, while in 1947 the snow was 45 feet deep in the cuttings and so hard-packed that it had to be blasted out with explosives. Photograph by kind permission of Mrs Pickersgill, Penrith.

Despite the difficulties, the railway was a wonderful invention allowing anything and everything to be moved more quickly, easily and cheaply. Barras Station was a busy place with carts to and fro all day. Mrs Pickersgill remembers vividly her arrival at Barras from Garrigill because of a peculiar coincidence:

We arrived at Barras Station at about quarter to twelve... the first people we

Two photographs taken at Stainmore Summit - above taking on water and, to the right, engine number 46475 heading east over Stainmore. The 46475 was a Class 2 Ivatt Mogul, an ex-LMS engine.

met... were a man called Mr Coulthard, who was the Station Master. Joe Hall who was thc son of James who farmed at Manor House, and he was also a signalman at Belah Cabin, and Mr Walton... and I remember my father saying, 'How funny, the last three people to see us away from Alston Station were also called Mr Walton, Mr Hall and Mr Coulthard.

Barras was said to be the station with the most beautiful view in the whole country, and originally the Station House, built in 1861, was an hotel, presumably to accommodate the expected tourists. In 1885 an article about Stainmore notes: 'If, indeed, its beauties and its treasures of mineral waters were more generally known, it might run the risk of becoming a fashionable resort.' The tourist trade however tended to rush past, gazing at the 'beauties' through their carriage windows en route from Newcastle to Blackpool.

Mr Atkinson lived at Tufton Lodge during the First World War and remembers hearing, 'the Germans bombarding West Hartlepool, early one morning.' Fears were very real, even as far away from anywhere as Stainmore. The Belah Viaduct was a possible German target and so, he said, 'During the War there were people there guarding it. They used to lodge at our house some on them, same way as when they used to paint it.' Ironically less than 50 years later the fine stone viaduct at Mousegill was blown to pieces by the British Army. A sad day indeed which, in retrospect, seems short-sighted.

Barras Station was closed in 1962 and work began to pull up the 100-year-old railway line. The famous Belah Viaduct which had cost £31,630 and the efforts of 80 navvies was demolished by a contractor from Coxhoe, County Durham. The metal had scrap value and so after being cut and dropped to the bottom of the gill it was hauled out again by crane. It took longer to demolish than it had taken to build, and the scrap value was certainly less than £31,630 and what of the labours of the 80 men? It was the demolition of a work of art.

Local people, powerless as ever against the great tides of progress, came out sadly to watch the destruction. Mr Alderson, of Barras Farm, seems to sum up the helpless feeling. In the words of a *Cumberand and Westmorland Herald* report he 'told his wife Edith, he could not bear to see the bridge destroyed, and went off to rebuild a bit of stone wall as if by way of recompense for the destruction of a familiar landmark.'

Early 1960s - removing rails from the Stainmore line up near the Summit.

The Belah Viaduct during demolition in 1963, with Tufton Lodge in the background. The viaduct had stood for 103 years, unlike one of its sister designs, the bridge over the River Tay in Scotland, also by Sir Thomas Bouch. The River Tay viaduct collapsed only two years after it was built while a train was crossing, causing the loss of about 80 lives. Photograph by kind permission of Mr Atkinson, Murton.

The view south over the Belah Viaduct as the rails were being lifted and before the viaduct was finally demolished.

The new Summit Sign which was put up to celebrate the 150th anniversary of the line by the Stainmore Railway Company Ltd. Photograph by kind permission of Mark Keefe.

The Plains of Heaven

High up on Barras Side
I stand to view the scene
And ask can they be real,
Or is it just a dream?

For 'tis here John Martin stood
To paint 'The Plains of Heaven'
And sure no grander scene
To mortals ere was given.

This poem was written by Revd. T. Westgarth, Vicar of Stainmore, who also took a lot of the photographs which have been used in this book. His daughter Ella Pickersgill from Eamont Bridge, kindly allowed the images to be used. I would like to say thank you to all the photographers who have contributed to this book, though often they are unknown. Thank you too to the many people who shared their memories - without them this book would have been impossible.

Dawn Robertson was born at Kings Meaburn, and educated at Appleby Grammar School and Sussex University. She worked at Newcastle University before returning to Cumbria where she was a journalist for the *Cumberland and Westmorland Herald.*

Over the years she has written several books and, for the last ten years has run Hayloft Publishing Ltd. *The Plains of Heaven* was originally published as part of a research project at Lancaster University and has long been out of print. She was first inspired to find out about the history of Stainmore after checking in several historical reference books, and finding the only reference to the parish was - the Romans arrived around 66AD - something must have happened since then, she thought, and so the research began.

By the same author:

Secrets and Legends of Old Westmorland
Riding the Stang
The Great Flood
A Country Doctor